THE POLITICS
OF THE GOSPEL

THE POLITICS OF THE GOSPEL

Jean-Marie Paupert

Foreword by Daniel Berrigan, S.J.

Holt, Rinehart and Winston
New York   Chicago   San Francisco

To all those who are laboring, whether by thought or action, for the coming of the Kingdom of God on earth as it is in Heaven,
and especially, because of his value as an example in my eyes, to Father Jacques Deparis,
I fraternally dedicate these pages.

J.-M.P.

Translated from the French by Gregor Roy

Grateful acknowledgment is made to the following publishers who have so generously granted permission to reprint from their publication: Excerpts from *The Jerusalem Bible*, copyright © 1966 by Darton, Longman & Todd, Ltd. and Doubleday & Company, Inc. Used by permission of the publishers.

Designer: Berry Eitel
SBN: 03-171725-6
Printed in the United States of America

Contents

Foreword

Daniel Berrigan was asked to write a foreword to this book because it seemed obvious that he would welcome its central thesis that fidelity to the Gospel implies a fundamental political orientation. His name would also suggest to readers that the book was not being offered as simply another theoretical statement, but was intended to lead to choices which could involve us in painful opposition to authorities of both Church and State. Because Father Berrigan is a poet, however, his foreword would be viewed as a simple call to activism, and because he makes no claim to be a political expert, his reflections would not be misunderstood as "authoritative" or necessarily excluding other responses, other forms of political witness.

The reader should not expect the Foreword to provide an analysis of Paupert's argument; he should look only for a personal word, set down at a particular moment (the end of 1968), from someone whose vocation has been to find new ways to proclaim the supreme relevance of the Gospel—to Vietnam, Black Power, and the growing gap between the rich and poor nations. It may be that by the time this book is published, Father Berrigan will be in jail; the forces of "law and order" will have been upheld against him and those other members of the "Catonsville 9" who "invaded" the Catonsville, Maryland draft board one day last spring and burned (with the help of homemade napalm, manufactured according to the instructions of the latest Army Field Manual) hundreds of draft records. Of course, it would be dishonest to pretend that many, even among Father Berrigan's friends, were not shocked by this action, but whatever the argument as to its symbolism and effectiveness, it suggested an even more disturbing question: would we not be even more shocked if we looked freshly at the politics of the Gospel?

The Editor

Our sour, despoiled hearts will perhaps name the year just past, if indeed we survive to name it, according to what we have suffered or inflicted on others. Will 1968 one day be called "The Year of Despoilment"? Or, shall we name it with a Chinese edge, "The Year of the Apotheosis and Decline of Our Most Exalted Leader Brought Low"? Or, from the point of view of the Church, "The Year of the Pill Denied"? Or, perhaps, "The Year of the Further Obfuscated"? Or will it be "The Year in Which the Past Was Affirmed With a Vengeance"?

In any case, reflection follows upon the losses and gains which the year brought—reflection upon infamy, violent death, unexplainable and opaque destiny, and, finally, reflection upon absurdity.

For example, in Thailand only a few weeks ago we of the West offered one of our few unequivocal gifts to the East— the death of Thomas Merton in Bangkok. He had stopped there on one stage of his first trip to the East, and he had determined to establish contact with Buddhist, Hindu, and Christian religious leaders in those cultures. At a time when political and social activism is the rage among western Christians, Merton had calmly turned his back (for a time, we trusted, and only to a degree) on all of that, and on all of us

as well. He undertook a search for alternatives; rightly understood, it was a revolutionary decision.

His death was particularly ironic and tragic for nine of us,
who some months before had been shockingly activist in
Catonsville, Maryland. In consequence of it, we had received a
particularly hard rap on the knuckles; our freedom is to be
denied us for some two and one-half to six years, the sentences
depending on the degree of leadership and conspiratorial in-
genuity presumably displayed by each.

As far as our trial was concerned, from every point of
view it had gone well. The pictures of those days show the
nine of us grinning like warlocks; our people were in the
streets, there were fiery evening sessions at old St. Ignatius
Church in Baltimore; national figures, students, priests and
hippies lined up to see the courtroom drama. By all accounts,
people were turned around, even the judges and the marshals.
For the peace movement, our trial seemed one of the few
events worth recording in an autumn that offered little encouragement. In Baltimore for one week men marched once
more, spoke out, shared their passion, and took hope. No one
was harmed or eaten.

During the trial, we of course had hoped for Merton's
presence. In prior instances, he had come, even though a
stage behind us, to see and support whatever actions we were
taking, from the early draft card burnings to the blood and
fire ceremonies in Maryland. If he was, indeed, a stage after
us, it should be understood that a monastery like Gethsemane
is not designed by nature or by grace for the forging of
radical Christian activists during war. The fact that Merton
struggled to understand and support us is vindicated now, in
an entirely new way, in my somber efforts at understanding
his death. His life operated on several fronts; every one of his
operations was in favor of peace. Within his own community
he had for some years stood apart from the "make work for
monks" mentality which marked so much of the monastery
routine. He was a figure of protest and of peace among his
own brethren; during the last few years, he lived apart in the

woods, writing and reading. One was reminded of the phrase of Bloy, "awaiting the Cossacks and the Holy Ghost."

I have no intention at such a time as this of eulogizing Merton and making cruel remarks about his brethren. We can only be grateful to those whose lives nurtured his for so many years. All of us, moreover, have suffered a mortal blow, the amputation from our body of a most sensitive and courageous man. Shall we, in our nearly blind grief, call him our eyes, our hands, our mouths? But I do not trust myself, at this point, to uncover the meaning of his loss to me. That loss came in installments, one grief riding another. A few days after his death I spoke to a friend, a writer, to whom I had been in the process of introducing Merton by letter. She was interested in undertaking a serious evaluation of his work and was prepared to fly to India or to Indonesia immediately in order to interview him at length. Then came the incomprehensible news, and she came to realize in the days that followed that the project of studying Merton in the midst of the enormous changes he himself had initiated in the Church was now ended. She was not interested, in other words, in an obituary.

We needed Merton at our trial. We needed him when the first resister was locked up. We needed him when King was murdered and the cities were aflame. We needed him at Selma and Montgomery. We needed him in somewhat the way we need a good hand, an ear, an eye—as a part of the body, without whom the body is crippled or sightless. And how many times in the months and years ahead, we will have cause to repeat that word of need! The western technological machine, bred out of Kafka or Verne, plays itself to exhaustion. The best men are cruelly assailed, the worst are engulfed in their own delusions of despair or grandeur—or murder. There are so few who can offer a simple, sane, and winning alternative to the universal method of death, the one infallible social and personal "solution." Has not in fact the Dachau method now been internationalized, from Hiroshima, through Vietnam, and on to Biafra? Indeed we found a late refinement in the Green Beret handbook on the making of simple, two-ingredient napalm. Our crime of course, was to misapply the "application;" paper instead of flesh.

If a threnody for Thomas Merton has point here, and indeed I am convinced that it does, its relevance lies in a simple truth: his life and death embody those ways of being a man which are the Christian options of Paupert's book.

Merton was a political man. His manifesto was the Gospel. He ranged the wilderness of his lifetime in possession of a center, a vision, and in possession of himself. As he grew up, he grew away from everything that was false and partial and merely accretive in religion. His growth was in another direction than that of mere piety or cultural consciousness, as his death in so distant a place and in so different a culture testifies dramatically. One is perhaps closer to the truth in saying he grew into the world.

Such a phrase, however, must be used precisely in deference to the precise thought of Jean-Marie Paupert. For Merton was in the world, not as one who draws upon this or that discipline or as a kind of "resource" person addicted to seminars or status. Rather, he was much given to the dignity of silence. He was, perhaps at his deepest, a man of tradition. According to that tradition, the world and those who make it up stand under the scrutiny of God. The Gospel allowed him sufficient light to follow the clues that lie hidden, unrecognized, and unconnected in the labyrinth of modern life. He followed through; he tracked down the beast. He was a merciless exorcist of the legions of devils that plague the soul of man and invade his body. War and its rhetoric, racism, nationalistic pride, the clichés of the establishment, the seductive revolutionary jargon of the leftist—all was grist for his vision.

It seems to me, in a time of grief, that the life of Merton stands as a kind of miraculous frontispiece to Paupert's book. And if I may be allowed to speculate on something which only time can clarify, perhaps Catonsville and our trial and imprisonment may someday take their place at Merton's side, according to a law which unites the most disparate actions if only they stand true to man.

"Was not your action merely symbolic?" they often ask us, with that uneasy puzzled eye men reserve for the antics of children or tame animals.

No. It was symbolic because it was political, and vice versa. Perhaps the equation is worth examining.

We were in agreement with the thesis of this book. We tried to explore it sometime before it was formulated so clearly, at least in this country. The book therefore invites further reflection of what we tried to do in May of 1968.

The creation of symbols and symbolic ways of acting has to do with the achievement of the public good. That is to say, when one acts publicly in a resisting or an illegal way, and when that act is nonviolent in principle, and when it is *new*, then we are justified in calling it an "exercise in consciousness," played out in public. Such symbolic action aims to communicate in a new way the force of the truths by which men live— if indeed they are to live at all. Among these truths, if one may be allowed to drag weighty matters over old ground, is the truth that life is a value which is slightly more precious than death.

Symbolic activity, consequently, aims to show forth or celebrate the slight edge which life has over death. Moreover, it aims to suggest that the pursuit of life—in all its variety and alternatives, in its imaginative branching out, in its defense under risk, in its capacity for creation of all kinds, in its spectrum of virtues and delights—is a more human and valuable enterprise than the pursuit of death.

From another point of view, such actions aim to point out the endless variety of the forms which life takes when men are reasonable and joyful and free. One thinks of sanity, courage, good humor, art, loving friendship, and converse. These are to be watched carefully, for, like good clues, they lead through experience into a new kind of innocence.

Americans, of course, are innocent. But their innocence is not the result of an experience of the real world. Their innocence has little to do with the profound inner life of a Merton or with his compassionate, surgical skill in diagnosing man's illness. American innocence is, rather, a compound that

includes ignorance, fear, isolation of spirit, and accumulated
suspicion of human variety, all based on 150 years of domestic
racism. At home and abroad today, this innocence is a political delusion, intoxicating and nearly incurable. Abroad, in its
military or paramilitary implications, it is necessarily lethal. It
literally cannot imagine its far-reaching consequences.

I saw such innocence in the three airmen whose release we
arranged a year ago in Hanoi. I saw the same innocence once
more in the astronauts who during this past month circled the
moon. During the week in which they orbited and returned to
earth, intoning the majestic cadences of the book of Genesis,
an American corporation announced that it had completed the
scientific preliminaries toward the orbiting of military space
stations. In short, the meaning of NASA, Bible reading aside,
is military; the arms race is now extended to include control
of the space race.

This politics of innocence is necessarily abstract. In contrast to it, as Paupert points out so admirably, the Gospel
conveys the stubborn rhythms, the starts and stops, the malice,
anxiety, pleasure, contentment, and fury of actual men. The
Gospel takes men into account in order to heal and bring
order. But American "ethical" conduct cannot imagine any
form of social life other than the "best" already achieved here.
The same order of things is therefore to be achieved elsewhere,
as the highest expression of what man can attain. By such a
simple, deadly extrapolation of a dubious domestic good,
innocence becomes threatening to all. No societal life can
express itself, at its own speed, according to its own rhythms
and symbols, with its own mind and heart intact.

The subject of imagination seems to me to lie at the heart
of Paupert's book because the Gospel *is* imaginative. It is therefore revolutionary, raising the question and encouraging its
open discussion—the question of how one is to be a man today.

The Gospel Paupert analyzes is, in the nature of things, a
political document. That is to say, it aims to serve consciousness, to awaken men to the alternatives which enlightenment
opens to them. It is not an exercise in delusion or selfishness
or transcendence. And this I take it is one of the simple and

important intuitions of this book. It gathers together the Gospel data, the first generation experience of Jesus by a community which had been faithful to His vision. It brings the data beyond the immediate circumstance of its composition into the scene where it belongs, that is to say, into the contemporary political and economic scene.

Thus Paupert is able to raise a question which is very old and quite central: is faith in Jesus of any public importance today? Or, more deeply, does the drama of death and victory played out in His flesh have any point for us; is it a center from which issue new signs and beginnings and evidences of life, even political points of departure? Are Christians justified in believing that their actions will bear fruit in political forms which express the hope of God for the community of man?

When the question of the political implications of the Gospel is placed in this way, it seems to me that the Gospel itself is relieved of the irrelevant burden so constantly placed upon it by misinformed Christians. Only a slavish spirit, after all, will overload the back of an ass over a long haul— especially when, as in Balaam's case, the ass raised its voice, a humble animal with the good sense of an angel. I dare say we know the dreary lading note of the muleteer—effectiveness, pride of place, wealth, the numbers game, obsessive moralizing on this or that theme.

No, the political implication of the Gospel is indeed something other than a burden placed upon it by those who wish to work it to death, to serve their own ends. Misused in such a way, the Gospel will not work at all. But neither will it die. Pseudo-spiritual, carnal, military, dictatorial, or pseudo-moralistic forms of life may drive the Gospel underground and all but annihilate it. The community of faith itself may betray or barter it away. Its spirit may be broken under the burden of law, an institutional slavery placed upon it by an authority fashioned by this world.

All of this in the long run, of course, makes no difference to the integrity of God's word. Indeed, whatever malice and blindness may attack the Gospel, subvert it, or deny it a hearing serves only to vindicate and enrich it. In every generation, a small number of believers wish to hear and obey. For them, the Gospel is the patience of God; it awaits the moment of hearing, a force of social regeneration—not according to the corrupt forms of men, but according to that power which is promised by the Holy Spirit.

It thus bears saying, as this book rightly insists, that the political power of the Gospel is of a different reality than the secular or cultural forces operating in the twentieth century. The Gospel is not to be seen as a resource of this or that time, an added quality or heightening of a life already intact. It is, rather, a kind of signatory power. It raises a sign of life and often, one sign among many. The sign declares that a serious work is underway, that a community is available to those who search and are hopeless or afflicted. The sign serves notice that an experiment is being made; a new chapter is underway in the common task of getting men moving toward justice, toward love, toward a new way of making change possible and coming upon alternatives to selfish or manipulative uses of power.

A work of partnership. Every attempt to raise the questions, to be true to human hope, is to be respected, talked with, drawn on, debated, included. It seems to me beyond doubt that *The Politics of the Gospel* could have been written only by a man who understands this and who has experienced the Church in conflict. Nor can the on-going debate exclude the most obvious current example of the possibility of a social communion. Such a possibility, of course, has long been neglected, ignored, and suppressed by an American political purpose. No more convenient solution could be imagined by religion and public polity, alike intent on the destruction of a common enemy. But it goes without saying that the results of such cold war crusading are nothing short of catastrophic to the nation and to the Church.

A recent poll, reported as a back page item in *The New York Times*, is instructive in this regard. America, we are told, is the society least equivocal among twelve nations studied in declaring its belief in God. At the same time, our "Christian" nation continues to pursue and "believe in" a war whose rake's progress has appalled the civilized world. Apparently, belief in our kind of God has sustained a military adventure justifiable neither by the Gospel, nor the Old Testament, nor by human conscience. "I believe, therefore I kill," is its apparent act of faith.

But the existence of an adversary to our religious and political suppositions, a community of atheists who might act as a critic to our cold war Church and State arrangement, who might challenge the existence of our national idolatries, and poke our closets until the armed skeletons rattled, such an adversary is a strict requirement of faith, a temper upon our Messianic drive, a brake upon our murderous righteousness. No such situation, however, obtains. The Communists are outlawed. We, believers and warriors, are alone in the field. The results are predictable. The effects of our use of power extend around the world and infect the other nations, east and west. The Russians enter into a gentlemen's agreement with us, balancing their project against the Czechs with our venture against the Vietnamese. Thus, too, the Chinese are driven to a more belligerent stand, the smaller nations seize on the atmosphere of meanness and strife for their own ends, and the Middle East erupts again and again. DeGaulle, whose *force de frappe* policies mark him as our partner in chaos, still has the perception to read the signs. "When the great powers indulge in violence as their ordinary method," he declared, "it is not to be wondered at that the smaller powers follow suit."

In such circumstances, it is entirely predictable that the political implications of faith are all but kneaded into a cultural mass. The leaders of the Church stand solidly with nationalism and its current madness and enlist in whatever violence or folly is underway. Their silence under crises, their prompt ratification in Christ's name of the old betraying bargain with Caesar, their backward looks at the well-being of their own back yards, their stolid inability to imagine what they might be as men, what they could contribute as citizens (and this precisely because they were Christians)—this is the old story of the American Church, written anew in the Vietnam years. Bishops, theologians, scholars, monks, laymen—

almost all arrive on the scene at the end of the action. They thereby miss the political point of the Gospel which is, I would think, that one arrives in the midst of the action in order to have a part in the action. The time being what it is, which is to say a time of total war on man, they arrive only to bury the dead.

In contrast, we find in the New Testament that Jesus came among men to rupture an ancient cyclic arrangement. According to its iron law, the innocent were simply plowed under; no transcendent vision could be invoked in their defense. Politics meant the expedient use of power, which is to say, power exists to favor only those who hold power.

But the life and death of Jesus justify the claim that He brought a new force into play against this evil and cynical order. The claim was made modestly, but it was boldly vindicated by His religious and social fervor, His love of the poor, and His tranquil joy in the face of the powers of death.

The record of historic Christendom, however, offers testimony. Once Jesus had safely ascended into Heaven, with embarrassing promptness Christians struck a bargain with the powers of this world. Dramatic political and symbolic actions, which might have made the kingdom of man ready for the Epiphany of God, were all but subsumed into the culture of the West. Such acts, of course, were never totally absent; indeed, their symbolism contained an astonishing power, enduring in artistic, political, and educational forms. Moreover, indirectly the Christian ethos humanized secular law and, to a degree, limited public violence. More directly and importantly the Spirit of Christ was embodied in a few men and women—ecstatics, heroes, martyrs, and heretics—whose lives testified to the power of a tradition.

It must, however, be admitted that in every stage of western development, the deepest impact of the Gospel was primarily cultural. That is to say, the impact of the Gospel as a transhistorical voice of "otherness," of transcendence, of ethical holiness and conscience, was consistently blunted and bargained away. Its revolutionary fervor was corrupted in the service of unregenerate men and their projects—world domination, colonialism, messianism, purity of blood, racism, war. Today we are witnesses of the newest and most terrible form of the old Christian-secular bargain—total and, from the point of view of the spirit, totalizing modern war.

Perhaps we are living out the last dying spasm of this long history. The American religious-civil arrangement, skillfully combining the threat of nuclear over-kill with an irresistible current of righteousness, is indeed all but impermeable against change. Pride and power at the center eye, and somewhere at the blind edge the despair of the nations, this conjunction of powers may well bring down the world. One does not know. Indeed, it must be said that one is forbidden to ask.

But this is the underside of the coin. The face of things lies in the filth and debris of history. Turn it up; the superscription says, "Trade in me." That is to say, "Be politically responsible; this is the currency of your faith in Jesus, the face of God stamped upon human metal. Live and die like Thomas Merton. Or burn the idols and go to jail for it."

When life and death are the evident issues, everything that otherwise seemed arbitrary or romantic must be taken into consideration once more. Indeed, the current romantic dream may be the supposition that change will occur through a "dressing up" of methods and structures that have already proved bankrupt—a change of administrators or engineers, a transfer of power, a new emperor in the old clothing. On the other hand, the height of political realism may be the supposition that a modest and self-giving action cuts the knot. The best reading of the times may mean, not that men take a new look at the old problems, with the old suppositions still in force, but that a few men are submissive before the mystery of hope. I believe, indeed, that this book invites us literally to take up and read an ancient document that can still speak to us with power, and we are asked to do so with an awareness of our hellish immediate geography. Having tried everything else, we might as well, in an act of trust which is very close to despair, try the Gospel.

Try it! The Church has tried almost everything else for nearly the whole of her historical existence, up to and including our current war and its perverse and corrupt messianism, the racist impasse of our parishes, our covert search for privilege and security, and the 1968 Christmas visit to bless our troops around the world. Everything has been tried; literally nothing has succeeded. We are coming at last to see that "religi-osified" culture is indeed an ossified culture, to the nth degree. And this is where we are. More property, more money, more power; and, at the same time, less suppleness, less quality, less resources of spirit.

All the projects and planning of the churches on behalf of social change, projects that drew consciously or otherwise on this world and this culture, have come to a dead halt. They were arbitrarily stamped as "Christian activity" merely because their authors were longing to save face and evade their own betrayals. But all of this has gotten nowhere, after years of over-publicized and frenetic experiments in "Church renewal."

The truth may lie in a totally different direction. We may as a people be living out on a larger scale that individual crisis of the young Augustine—part Christian and therefore wholly pagan. Man is sunk in despondency, at the end of his resources. If we are lucky, our despair may finally be invaded by an act of God. *Tolle et lege;* take up and read. There is but one book, as all men are but one man.

January, 1969   *Daniel Berrigan, S.J.*

INTRODUCTION:

For an Evangelical Politics

Why is our world in its present condition? Why, two thousand years after the Gospel, do we feel so much despair and live constantly in dread of wars and upheavals? Is it that the world is pagan? Perhaps. But the Good News has been proclaimed once and for all; it has resounded over the whole world; and since the death of Christ, at least in the West the moving force of civilization has largely coincided, both geographically and historically, with the preaching of the Gospel. What then?

Let us recall only some recent events, those that our contemporaries have known or their parents told them about (a modern chanson de geste for a long winter's night): during World War I Christian peoples confronted each other in a terrible butchery while at the same time some sons of Christendom traveled to the ends of the earth to preach peace and universal love. The first half of this century, like the last, has known streams of blood, hatred, and heartrending calamity—even internally within one nation—between oppressed and oppressors in the struggle that men might have enough to eat, that children might be properly cared

1

for, that women might live in dignity, and that everyone might be free. We have also known the horrors of Auschwitz and the holocaust of Hiroshima. Finally, there are the succulent and towering garbage heaps of rich nations (generally Christian) at the gates of countries where children have sad eyes and swollen bellies.

A few very sensible reminders should certainly allow us to avoid a facile and superficial disgrace. The Gospel remains a seed to be scattered over the earth; the Kingdom of God is not of this world; the time of the Church is that of the struggle (Lk 21: 29-36). Even in God's field, the enemy who sows cockle continues his work (Mt 13:24-30, 36-43), and each man knows that the field where the cockle and the good grain grow together is also his own heart and his own life. We might also recall the cutting irony with which Saint Paul greeted the dreams of earthly messianism that were fascinating the Corinthians.

Still another observation may calm our uneasiness for a moment. After all, is it not obvious that the wars, injustices, and horrors that have been cited—in general, the very evil of the modern world—are the fruit of a return to paganism? When all is said and done, Nazism was anti-Christian, and so is Marxism, and capitalism is equally materialistic.

If in the West all men and countries who profess to be Christian or are so by tradition really were Christian, all these past and present horrors could never have emerged.

To say this is to recognize the force of the Gospel of Jesus Christ, confided to the protection of the Church; but this is not the same as declaring Christians "not guilty." Indeed, when we think about it for a minute, guilt is perhaps the harshest accusation we could bring against ourselves. After all, it is a fact that the unchaining of the evil forces of war and injustice has been especially evident in those geographical areas either impregnated with Christianity or under the leadership of Christians. Recognition of this truth is painful and calls for a certain courage. The Christian people should nevertheless come to terms with it, whatever the cost. Then perhaps they will hear the heavy charges the prophets brought against Israel—which would be a way of making Biblical renewal a practical reality—as well as the voices and testimonies that have been given within the Church in order to awaken it and to which little attention has been paid. However, there is a new factor in our Christian history; faced with the spectacle of our denominational disunity, we are beginning to confess our sin. Should we not go a step further, however, and also recognize our responsibility in the face of the tragic situation in which the world and contemporary civilization finds itself? It is obvious, after all, that we bear a considerable share of guilt in this whole crisis. Is not such an admission the first attitude required of us as soon as we place ourselves with some seriousness before the Gospel and the agony of today's world? We will not cure the world by justifying ourselves, but perhaps we can begin to make a contribution to that cure by humbly taking the measure of our share of responsibility in the failure of our time and by trying to discover our duty with greater accuracy and resolution.

We believe, surely, that Christ has obtained victory over death and the powers of darkness and carries us with him in this victory. His Gospel, surely, is for us the Good News of our salvation and of what must be done in order to be saved; it is the sacrament of Truth and Life, both for us and for the entire world. But why, then, could paganism in all its guises be reborn after so many centuries of Christianity—and in the very womb of what was Christendom? Why is the Christianity that we officially profess so weak a force for justice, love, and peace when weighed against the great problems of the world—especially since it was such a great force in the early days of the Church? If the Gospel has not been sufficiently preached in terms of the realities of the day, if the testimony borne by the Christian people as a whole has not done justice to all its demands in the social and political domain, can we say that it has truly taken hold of our lives? This is the reproach we sense in the smiles and accusations of unbelievers around us. They force us into a dilemma: because we have not done more to transform the world in the image of the Kingdom of God, either the Gospel is not worth much or we have not really taken it seriously.

It is not easy to satisfy ourselves by using the paganized modern world as an alibi for our present evils. After all, this paganized world has emerged in the midst of Christendom, the responsibility of the Western world remains predominant, and for centuries it represented Christendom. Why this regression? Various aspects of those "Christian centuries" are, of course, under criticism from unbelievers, and their objections should keep us from chanting their praises too enthusiastically, even when we recognize the good fruits that have come in the past from the seed of the Gospel. Thus the critics might show us the growth of cockle in the excesses of feudalism, serfdom, various aspects of the Crusades, the very practice of pursuing religious objectives with military arms, the wars of princes and popes, and the Inquisition. Even if we do not want to emphasize these points, place them all on the same level, or judge them in terms of our contemporary sensibility, we know that the testimony of the Gospel was and still is burdened by these souvenirs, which can scarcely be said to illustrate the spirit of the Beatitudes.

Here again, let us try for a balanced presentation. The hearts of men are not changed in one day, or even in a century, or in ten. The conversion of hearts and of civilizations is a task that always needs to be renewed; it will never be achieved in a radical and definitive way. Can we deny that there has been progress in humanity and in the Church

—and in the first, thanks to the second? Is it not a little too easy to impute all the evil of the world to the indifference and the inaction of the bearers of the Gospel? Let us recognize instead the reality of moral progress, which is a long-range task but which a history of various world views and institutions cannot deny.

All these explanations, however, cannot dispel our uneasiness or resolve our problem. They remain because of the concomitance of two quite contradictory realities: our political situation, with its retinue of evils and injustices; and the preaching of the Gospel, which is a power for peace and love in the world. The contradiction is too flagrant for us to be able to avoid the disgrace it constitutes so long as we have not done everything in our power to overcome and suppress it. And have we truly done this, with realism, to the degree called for by the actual situations?

A definite improvement in Catholic attitudes during the last few years should also be pointed out. In most of the so-called developed nations Catholics no longer form a monolithic bloc in the continuing ideological and political struggle. But does not this liberation from total identification with a bloc or a party extend to the point of becoming a dangerous political liberalism? The question deserves to be raised in immediate terms as one of those in which something extremely serious is at stake. We have learned to respect all opinions—or almost all—and to consider the sphere of politics as a free field, closed on itself, where Christians and non-Christians can meet and confront each other without implicating faith but rather arguing in the name of one or another "ism." But have we sufficiently taken into account the possibility of a new risk? Adherence to ideological camps can take precedence over the demands of the Gospel or become a pretext to borrow the assumptions of Christian social thought for one's own use in order to conceal those options that do not flow from it. In this way injustices and crimes are committed in the name of political choices that are then linked up with faith. Unrelated positions insist on referring to the Gospel, the cross, and faith. The most formal texts are twisted in the direction of one's individual options, and Christians are apparently divided in the name of the same faith, the same Gospel. Christian themes become pretexts to cover impassioned choices or are used as excuses for inaction.

In this way during recent decades Christians have been divided in the name of Catholicism or Christian tradition or the Gospel—something that should be a unified whole. For or against the republic, for or against Dreyfus, anti-Semites or anti-anti-Semites, for or against the social laws, for or against Franco or Vichy, for or against the worker-priests, for or against Catholic schools, for or against the war in Vietnam or independence for Algeria, for or against torture—the political divisions of Christians are mingled with references to Christianity and constantly risk falsifying the Gospel and its demands, submitting it in a greater or lesser degree to partisan and ideological outlooks that are fundamentally foreign to its spirit.

There is a little of everything in these ambiguities, some inadmissible and some necessary. We deliberately refer to them in bulk in order to show the poverty of Christian consciousness today in the area of politics. Father Jolif, dean of studies at the Dominican seminary at Arbresle, has himself noted:

It is quite characteristic that, with a few rare exceptions, theologians have not yet come to think seriously about politics as such. In a widely used manual of moral theology,[1] two pages are enough to present the norms of political life. In them one learns that the civil power has the duty to watch over the gen-

[1] H. Jone, *Précis de théologie morale catholique* (1958), pp. 137–139. Of course, moral theology cannot be judged by one author, however universal!

eral good and that legislators should promote the common good in a positive manner. As for subjects, it is incumbent on them to love their country, respect authority, elect good representatives, and obey the laws in general and fiscal laws in particular (this last point occupies by itself half the space given to the whole subject). Finally, soldiers who have voluntarily entered service ought to fulfill their obligations and complete their enlistment. Confronted with such a treatise, it is no exaggeration to say that political theology, which underwent such magnificent developments in the sixteenth century, notably with Victoria, has not survived in the modern world. The political disturbances that accompanied the Algerian war have shown to what confusion the absence of reflection in this domain can yield.

Practice is hardly ahead of theory. The password of one bishop, "Avoid politics, which divides men, and rally around religion, which unites them," has not been an isolated attitude. Many sharp criticisms might be made regarding the behavior of numerous Christians who, under the fallacious pretext of charity, avoid those confrontations apart from which no value can be inscribed in history.[2]

All kinds of distinctions have been brought forward: the Christian and the citizen, Catholic action and political action, action as a Christian and action that is Christian. In spite of everything that may be valid in these refinements (as well as what may be provisional), such distinctions cannot take away from us one essential conviction: we are simply unfaithful to the Kingdom of Heaven when, proclaiming the same Credo and bearing witness to the same Gospel (which is entirely one), priests and Christians are divided on an *essential* political problem that is also a problem of Truth. Of course, many problems are open to varying judgments, but are they as numerous as is imagined and do they exist to the degree that is imagined? We do not happen to think so. Is faith sincere that does not act or

[2] J. Jolif, O.P., "L'Homme contre la société," *Economie et Humanisme* (September 1962), p. 14.

whose action does not proceed to the end—that is, even in its political implications? Has it become incarnate? More simply but perhaps more brutally, is the same Gospel able to leave us free to be for or against the same war? Were Christians clearheaded in 1914, when on both sides of the front that separated them they justified, often with the greatest enthusiasm, the value of the war they waged against each other? Was the drama of Benedict XV that of Christians in general at that time? In the face of such facts, what should those who do not believe that the Lord has truly died and risen again think of our faith? Will it not seem to them some kind of spiritual luxury? Will the Gospel as lived by Christians be for them a question or a call?

There is no question here of immediately resolving questions of such scope or even of posing them in all their sharpness or with all the relevant data. But it is necessary from the outset to indicate how great the problem is. Where does the difficulty come from? Would it not be due first to the fact that Christians, more than suffering a failure of heart or of good will, have not been sufficiently enlightened on this subject, have not sufficiently taken into account what is spiritually at stake in political action?

Our intention is first to clarify historically how this problem has arisen. We shall examine early Christianity's behavior in political matters. Next we shall see how, in the complexity of history, the status that the Church adopts in the course of its development determines the clarity of the problem in the conscience of Christians. It seems to us that at the present time the evolution of the Church's role in various countries and a fervent interior renewal are causing it to rediscover the essentially evangelical conditions of political commitment. Vatican II was a turning point; we can now take a better reading and uncover basic requirements of such a commitment. But it is necessary, first, to agree on the word "politics." The term must be seized in its breadth and all its rigor. There can be no question of doubly reducing the field of our study—first, from the temporal point of view, to the interaction of political parties, tendencies, structures, and administrations that converge or have converged in the government; then, from the theological point of view, to the question of relations between Church and State.

In fact, it is appropriate to understand "politics" in the full meaning it retains from the Greek, which makes it applicable to everything that formerly concerned the organization of the city (*polis*)—that is, really to everything that depends on and flows from the social life of man. Philologically, as well as logically and philosophically, the words "social" and "political" cannot be unduly separated, as if one were concerned simply with human relationships (familial and professional) within the nation and the other, with the problems of national government and international relations. In fact, a healthy view of things, according to the etymology that makes the Greek *politeia* very close to the Latin *societas*, impels us to become aware that everything that is social is political, and vice versa. To be more precise, regardless of the necessity and legitimacy of the economic, social, and moral points of view (or formal purposes) of the communitarian human reality, "politics" includes them all and is, therefore, as Aristotle well saw, the supreme activity and science of man. Saint Thomas himself, from the purely human point of view, consented to this primacy, of which it was ultimately deprived by theology alone.

Consequently, our political study from the Christian and, more precisely, evangelical point of view will not be limited to the important issue of the relations between

Church and State, between the spiritual and the temporal. This issue, however significant, is only one element in our overall subject.

To put it quite simply, our intention is to answer the following three questions:

—What has Christ recommended in his preaching concerning the social relations of men?

—How do these prescriptions find their way or become blurred in the minds of Christians in accordance with the working rules that the Church finds or adopts in the world during the course of history?

—Which are the key points of contemporary awareness and within which challenges and fundamental positions are they to be found?

Then we shall have to present our conclusion.

To be able to respond, at least briefly, to these questions, we shall first examine the evangelical text itself. It should hardly be necessary to show exactly why this preeminence and privileged status is to be given to the Gospel; the reason should be quite self-evident.

The Gospel does not simply represent a particular period of Christianity but is at the very center of Christian Revelation. It is, first, a doctrine, a "tradition" that was soon crystallized in scripture; as such, its implications are certainly capable of development but not rejection; they may follow a homogeneous but not a heterogeneous evolution. In the course of time they cannot be made to change from white to black, from yes to no, from against to for. Accommodations to life can take place, as well as transformations of historic relationships, but there cannot be a negation of the very essence of the Gospel. We may go even further. The Gospel is not simply a tradition; in a sense it is *the* Tradition—in that it is the written record that concretizes the primitive tradition based on Christ's preaching, the very Son and Word of God. It is the hinge of Revelation, the conclusion of the Old Alliance, and the beginning of the New. And it is all this right from the beginning, once and for all—like a living cell that holds at once, in its complex simplicity, the best physical and chemical substances, the surest hereditary gifts of both near and remote ancestors, as well as all the potentialities of the future. We are well advised, therefore, to examine the Gospel with special devotion in connection with our present undertaking.

Having done this, we shall attempt, by drawing on a few key witnesses, to set out in a schematic manner the place of evangelical political doctrine in the various periods of the Church and of the Western world. Our attitude will appear critical for two reasons: we shall analyze these special examples in light of today's discoveries rather than in terms of the problems of their own age, and we are especially anxious to make today's Christians see that their orientation in this area is surrounded by risks about which they should try to be extremely clear. My intention is that reflection on history also be an appeal for greater perceptiveness.

We then come to the immediately contemporary period, to which, one can easily understand, we give special emphasis. In particular we shall analyze several of the problems—more or less false, more or less true—that make up, or have recently been major themes of, modern Christian political thought (monarchy and republic, right and left, socialism and capitalism, the crisis of the worker-priests) and confront the difficulties they contain with the data of evangelical thought.

By way of conclusion, we then can propose a few synthetic views and some proposals for immediate action.

It can be seen at once that we are not pretending to write a treatise, even a short one, on Christian sociopolitical morality. Our intention will be considered more or less ambitious, depending on the attitude of the individual. It is nothing less than a plea for an evangelical politics.

This little book is greatly indebted to all those who, especially in recent decades, have struggled in order that the Kingdom of God be established on earth as it is in Heaven. The author believes, not without some immodesty, that this struggle has not yet clarified the orientations that ought to be essential for the Christian. This book does not pretend to furnish them. It is an essay, and as such it wishes to serve as a catalytic agent for people who are actually engaged in this effort. If it ignores certain nuances, it does not intend to deny them. But its purpose is, first of all, to make people react, so that essential questions may be seen for what they are. The book has not been written as a thesis but as a proposal on which to center the continuing debate.

I
THE TEACHING
OF JESUS

1

THE POLITICAL LIFE OF JESUS

"Christian" is said of Christ. Christ, a man born during the reign of Caesar Augustus in a small village of a Roman colony, lived more or less obscurely for thirty years or so in the home of a carpenter named Joseph, who passed as his father. His mother was named Mary, and he himself was called Jesus. In the company of some disciples, poor and simple folk, mostly fishermen, he left his parents to preach a doctrine of salvation. In support of his preaching, he performed, according to evangelical tradition, those marvels that are called miracles.

What he said was very simple but a little mysterious. Besides, for the most part he spoke in parables—in the spirit of these ancient Oriental peoples, he told little stories whose meaning, both apparent and hidden, constituted his teaching. He often spoke of his Father who had sent him, and who was not Joseph, because he was "my Father in Heaven." He also spoke of Another whom he would send, a protector and interpreter. He spoke especially of a kingdom, which was not precisely that of Israel but "the Kingdom of Heaven," a kingdom open to the poor, the meek, and the sinful, a kingdom whose laws were neither those of Moses (without, however, excluding them) nor those of the Roman occupation but an ensemble of paradoxical and extraordinary prescriptions dominated by an extravagant Love of God. He was frequently in opposition to the theocratic leaders of his people, reproaching them for their pride, their compromises, their hypocrisy, their formalism, and their hardness of heart; he welcomed and favored the poor and the outcasts of the nation; he spoke with ambiguity about himself as the Son of Man, the Son of God, and the Son of David, the Messiah who was heir to the throne of the great king. Consequently the leaders of the priests, scribes, doctors of the law, and elders of the people, finally exasperated, had no great difficulty in condemning him, according to their terms, as impious and sacrilegious (we would say heretical) and in having him condemned, for external usage, by the Roman occupying authorities, as a revolutionary, an enemy agitator to the de facto power. At only a little more than thirty years old, he was therefore crucified, in the midst of general tumult and unrest, which was frequent in these areas during holidays. This all took place under Tiberius; Pontius Pilate was procurator of Judea.

At first all this does not appear to represent the outlines of a great leader or of a powerful political message, but the perspective changes if things are looked at a little more closely.

The Palestinian Background

It would be appropriate, to begin with, to recall that Jesus, because of his Jewish birth, was heir to the century-old political tradition of Israel, which we may briefly define as theocracy. Apart from a few nuances, politics and religion very nearly coincided; it was Yahweh Himself who, by means of patriarchs, judges, kings, and prophets, governs His chosen people. The "civil" law of the people has an intrinsically religious meaning by the very fact of election, and even the most religious regulations, those concerning prayer and worship, have the force of civil law. In addition, the exclusive Yahwism of the Hebrew nation, which was a response to God's election, marked it strongly with nationalism. Quite naturally, the awaited Messiah will be a spiritual and temporal savior, almost without distinction.

The political situation in Christ's time is well known. Palestine itself was occupied either directly (Judea, Samaria) or indirectly (Galilee, Peraea) by the Romans, who demanded tribute from the colonies but respected their religious entity and left the power of judging civil and religious cases to the seventy-one members of the Sanhedrin. The masses of the people, however, were in favor of resistance to the occupying authority.

On the social level, there were few direct struggles; slavery had been considerably lightened for some time, in accordance with the position of Deuteronomy (15:12–15):

If your fellow Hebrew, man or woman, is sold to you, he can serve you for six years. In the seventh year you must set him free, and in setting him free you must not let him go empty-handed. You must make him a generous provision from your flock, your threshing-floor, your winepress; as Yahweh your God has blessed you, so you must give to him. Remember that you were a slave in the land of Egypt and that Yahweh your God redeemed you; that is why I lay this charge on you today.

This nation of farmers, shepherds, and artisans was theocratically ruled by a handful of priests, Levites, and especially doctors of the law or scribes. Generally speaking, the latter belonged to the sect of Pharisees. Many of them held to a formalistic and juridical notion of morality, a scrupulously literal orthodoxy concerned with ancient traditions. They also had an extreme sense of nationalism, although this was always expressed in moderate terms, and their opposition to the Romans always showed respect for legal forms. They were conservatives.

They were surpassed in zeal by the Zealots, whose attitude managed to synthesize the extreme right and the extreme left; they were a little like a cross-breeding of national socialists and anarchists. For the most part they came from the lower classes and were as aggressively pious as they were fanatically nationalistic. The domination exercised over the people by the ruling classes, as well as the abandonment by the latter—with the exception of the Pharisees—of the rules of faith and practice and of plans for restoring the nation, brought the Zealots to such a point of exasperation that they did not hesitate to resort to direct action.

It is true that most priests belonged to the aristocratic sect (which also included laymen in its ranks) of the Sadducees. Under the combined influence of Greek thought and Biblical literalism, having recourse to written law at the expense of the cumbersome oral tradition, they had arrived at a certain degree of liberalism. They had reached a very satisfactory accommodation with the occupying authorities; they were distinguished people, liberals, and collaborators.

The Herodians were not so refined or so complicated; it is difficult even to know if they were for or against the Romans. What is certain is that they occasionally made limited alliances with the Pharisees and, above all, that they were entirely and blissfully devoted to the cause of Herod, "the fox." The rest had little importance for them.

In a country with such a theocratic structure, it was natural that most of the religious sects were also political forces. Nevertheless, there was one exception: the Essenes, who were entirely given over to prayer and asceticism, in an atmosphere of segregation, perhaps even of secrecy, and in any case with the deepest scorn for all material and social contingencies.

All these tendencies were certainly found again in the general expectation of a triumphant Messiah. The author of *The Assumption of Moses*, who was virtually a contemporary of Jesus, bore witness to this:

He rises up, the supreme God, the only eternal One, and He will manifest Himself in order to punish the nations, and He will destroy all their idols. Then you will be happy, Israel, and you will mount on the wings of the eagle. . . . And God will raise you up and place you in the Heaven of the stars. . . . And you will see your enemies on earth.

The Political Significance of the Life of Jesus

In this framework it is interesting to consider the political life of Jesus, first disregarding his logia as well as his formal teaching; concentrating only on how what he *did* stands out in relief against the context of his age establishes certain basic tendencies.

The first remarkable fact is that of the Incarnation: the Word of God, which has manifested its astonishing power in more than one instance, is also at the same time a man, solidly rooted and forcefully implanted in the soil of Palestine. We meet his parents and his friends; we see them living intimately in a very specific universe.[1] This positive Incarnation is the basic reason why Christianity will never be simply a disembodied spiritual philosophy, but can and ought to be political.

From our present point of view, let us be more precise and say that in the Gospel family life is evoked especially

[1] On this point see my *Quelle est donc cette Bonne Nouvelle?* (1961), pp. 29–37.

by reference to the bridegroom and the bride, the father and the mother, the home and its various parts—its roof, its door, its cellar, the clothes that are mended, the cloak, the bread that is baked, wine and salt, and such household objects as a pitcher, a lamp, a girdle, tables, liquor, and meals.

Social, economic, and political life, obviously including family life, is very widely represented in addition by the great attention given to such major events as births, holidays, mournings, and funerals. There are also frequent references to cities, palaces, the temple, the altars, and the baths; to occupations and classes (Pharisees, head waiters, soldiers and officers, merchants, vine growers, shepherds, fishermen, stewards, and superintendents) and their tools (thread, needles, hatchets, swords); to war, weddings, adultery, and all sorts of illness. We meet epileptics, bleeding women, men suffering from dropsy, lepers, the blind, the deaf, and the palsied; it is a walking "Court of Miracles," all taking place out of doors and giving us the real atmosphere of the Near East. Naturally, in these texts money plays an important part—as well as such precious objects as pearls, sometimes valued in terms appropriate for children's stories (the precious pearl, the buried treasure, the immense wealth), but more frequently associated with a fatal power, that of Mammon)—described under all its forms and emblems: minas, talents, staters, drachmas.

Someone might object that this whole arsenal, all this physical luggage, is simply the result of chance—that is, of the joint influences of the three social factors emphasized by Taine: race, environment, and period. And certainly, apart from what is unique, we would not deny this; one of the essential realities of the Gospel, we repeat, is the Incarnation; the Incarnate Word is not half a man, an appearance. But this does not make any the less true the fact that God chose to reveal himself to us in a context of reality that was very humble and simple, and has eminent social and political dimensions.

If we penetrate a little deeper into this reality, we notice that Jesus was born poor, even absurdly poor; he lived in the same way, surrounded by poor people as well as those who were especially disrespectable (prostitutes, publicans, and so on; see Lk 15:1). All this was done without righteousness or ostentation, for he also occasionally had dinner with the well-to-do.

The fact remains that the Word of God chose to be of the poorest of a poor people and in addition to live his whole life within the milieu of manual workers (his father, Joseph the carpenter—see Mk 6:3; Mt 13:55—his disciples, fishermen), the sick, and the disinherited. Let us also note that in a sociological context polarized by virility, Jesus reserved an important and very noble place in his life and action to women: first, to his mother, Mary; then to the sisters of his friend Lazarus, with whom he liked to converse; to widows; and in a general way to everything that women do. It is clear that he had observed their occupations with care—recall the account of the housekeeper's search for the missing coin (Lk 8:9) and the description of grinding grain (Lk 17:35; Mt 24:41); Jesus knew both their sorrows and their joy in giving birth to a child (Jn 16:21).

Jesus' attitude toward the established order was simple. In striking contrast with the frequent practices of his time, he was neither servile or obsequious nor scornful or aggressive toward the occupying authorities. In his relations with the procurator of Judea, there was a divine dignity, and he remained serenely himself throughout the trial (Jn 18:33–38, 19:9, 12); nor did he hesitate to cure the sick servant of the Roman centurion of Capernaum, whose manly faith received special praise. It is true that Luke (7:4–5), but not Matthew (8:5 ff.), specifies that this was at the insistent demand of the leaders of the local Jewish community because they argued that the occupying authority was a good man: " 'He deserves this of you,' they said, 'because he is friendly toward our people; in fact, he is the one who built the synagogue.' "

On the other hand, the behavior of Christ is already more severe toward Herod, the tetrarch of Galilee, who nevertheless was, like Pilate, the bearer of an exclusively temporal power. But Jesus, let us keep in mind, did not like political opportunism. In addition to Herod's many vile actions, Jesus doubtless could not forget that this unscrupulous careerism had been a betrayal of the chosen people to which he belonged. He had only disdain and scorn for this man who wished to kill him (Lk 13:32); Herod was "the fox" (Lk 13:32) before whom, and before whom alone, he would not condescend even to open his mouth during his passion (Lk 23:9), whereas he tried to explain himself before Pilate and even before the Sanhedrin.

This is not to say that Jesus had any tenderness for that high court, any more than for the scribes and doctors or any of the party sects—that is, for any of these politicoreligious structures—in which, however, he had quite a few friends, but as individuals, including Simon the Pharisee, Nicodemus, and Joseph of Arimathea. Christ was unable to be in complete harmony with any of the groups—neither with the Pharisees, whom he scourged so violently and frequently, especially in Matthew 23 (this whole chapter is filled with anathemas and sarcasm: "Alas for you, scribes and Pharisees, you hypocrites! . . . whitewashed tombs . . . brood of vipers"); nor with the Zealots, who could not be satisfied, for example, with the solution Jesus brought to the problem of tribute (Mk 12:13 ff.; Mt 22:15 ff.; Lk 20:20 ff.); and clearly not with the Herodians, who were allied with the Pharisees on the question of tribute.

In addition, some essential points of evangelical doctrine should be seen as in fundamental opposition to the spirit of these sects, taken either as a whole or separately. For example, the universalism of the evangelical vocation was not a feature of any of them; its elements of simplicity and emphasis on social transformation only alienated the aristocratic parties, the Sadducees and Pharisees, who preferred order and domination to love, and would rather establish barriers than suppress them. Besides, the Sadducees could not accept the doctrinal rigor of Christ, whereas the Pharisees instinctively rejected his revision of theological values to give predominance to faith, love, and will. As for the Zealots, how could they forgive Christ his reformism, which was not directly revolutionary (in the political sense), his faith in the conversion of hearts, and his political indifferentism (at least in appearance), which led him to introduce the ferment of transformation rather than attempt the immediate realization of revolution?

To all these politicians, what did it matter that the coming of the Kingdom of God, as Jesus conceived it, was one of the central elements of evangelical preaching?

In fact, it is in regard to this problem of the Kingdom and of kingship that everything was to be decided. The political and the religious were to reunite for the final climax. With the exception of Jesus, everyone lost his bearings during this politicoreligious trial, in this tale of royalty —especially Pilate, who wanted to preserve his good conscience, and those Jewish leaders, who had both good faith and bad faith. The members of the council of elders, the scribes, the high priests, and the members of the Sanhedrin, after convincing themselves that Jesus was really saying that he was the Son of God (Mk 14:61, 62; Lk 22:67, 71; Mt 26:63, 65), presented their accusation before Pilate on a triple basis: "We have found this man inciting our people to revolt, opposing payment of the tribute to Caesar, and claiming to be Christ, a king." (Lk 23:2).

The first point was true but ambiguous, as was the third, and the second charge was clearly false. It is quite obvious that when someone begins to preach in the towns and villages, declaring that everything is not for the best in the best of all possible worlds, calling for reform, criticizing the powerful, and haranguing crowds, he will give rise to a certain excitement and even some degree of agitation. But all this can be called disorder only if we think of order in police terms. In this way we can see that in Jesus' case (which is extremely interesting in the framework of this book's general argument) there already had taken place this defense mechanism on behalf of the established powers that tends to stigmatize as disorder (of a minor nature, like a street fight) what is actually a struggle against profound disorder. Too often, those who talk the most about the word "order" possess it the least—which is also true of "liberty."

When they accused Jesus of presenting himself as Christ the king, the Hebrew leaders knew very well that they were playing with words and how they were playing with them. They took what for them was essentially heretical (although involving a heresy that was of equal concern to the temporal order, which was only natural in a theocracy) and presented it to the procurator in a framework that was essentially political, in the Roman sense of the term. Indeed, during the trial they emphasized this distortion more and more. Pilate, who was neither stupid nor very likely to be ignorant about Judaism defended himself very well; he first insisted that the whole thing was one of those civil-religious affairs peculiar to the Jews that they were used to handling: "Take him yourselves, and try him by your own Law" (Jn 18:31). Constrained, nevertheless, to handle the case himself, he was quickly impressed by Jesus. Even a brief interrogation was enough to convince Herod that he was not deceived and that if this man really called himself the King of the Jews, the title contained nothing to worry his master, Tiberius (Mk 15:2; Mt 20:7, 11; Jn 18:33–38), and he said so. But the enemies of Jesus renewed their attack, pursuing a skillful policy by provisionally abandoning the question of royalty and insisting again on disorder: "He is inflaming the people with his teaching all over Judea; it has come all the way from Galilee, where he started, down to here" (Lk 23:5). The flimsy reference to Galilee provided the basis for the useless and grotesque encounter with Herod; after this, Pilate, still concerned to save Jesus, tried to make use of the right of *abolitio* in his favor, by placing him in balance with Barabbas.

At this point the situation became more complicated. Although John (18:40) refers to this Barabbas as a brigand, if kept in mind his imprisonment by the Roman authorities, it seems more likely that he was active in the resistance to the occupation. This was also Father Lagrange's opinion. Barabbas was probably a member of the Zealots, a supposition that would not be contradicted by the account in John, because the Zealots, like everyone in the resistance, found themselves or believed themselves obliged, in order to eat, to have recourse to extortions—at the expense of both the Roman garrisons and their compatriots, which prevented them from living like little altar boys or having a very good reputation. Opinions about them would have been especially negative because reprisals exacted against their operations affected one and all. Thus, Pilate thought himself very clever to propose the *abolitio* in favor of the popular Jesus on the occasion of Passover. He believed he could take advantage of the Jewish leaders by putting them in opposition to the populace, who were sympathetic to Jesus and always ready to become aroused by the old Messianic dreams while simultaneously ridiculing once more the politicoreligious pretensions of Judaism and showing that for him the whole business remained internal to their system. It was quite deliberately, therefore, that he presented Jesus to them several times as "the King of the Jews" (Mk 15:9, 12;

Mt 27:17, 22; Jn 18:39). It was a clever game, but it was a little bit too clever; what he forgot was that in this instance the elders and the scribes, because of the importance of what was at stake, could forget their former animosity to the Zealots (who could scarcely count on having friends among the scribes and Pharisees or among the Sadducees or, in general, among the upper classes) and could think, on the contrary, that Pilate would be doubly provoked to see Jesus (who was no bother to him) condemned and Barabbas (an authentic danger for the Pax Romana of the country) liberated—not to mention the fact that a Barabbas liberated thanks to these leaders would be more or less their prisoner. Fine, the political deal would be even better than before, thanks to this booby Pilate! The latter forgot, besides, that the psychology of crowds is extremely subtle and requires the most delicate handling, enlightened by a profound knowledge of the psychological forces and socio-cultural tendencies at work. But as Father Lagrange said:

The Messiah in chains before a Roman procurator evoked such a grotesque idea in the eyes of the Jews that those very people who had previously held great hopes of him suddenly experienced a disenchantment that turned into anger. Perhaps those who pitied Jesus were also given to understand that he would be able to surmount his problems in another way, whereas Barabbas, a hero of the independence movement, was in very serious danger!

The case was now lost; from then on, Pilate only engaged in delaying tactics. First, there was the scourging, then the crowning with thorns and the public mockery—still *royal*, we should note: "Hail, King of the Jews!" (Mk 15:18; Mt 27:29; Jn 19:3). The procurator was obstinate, and it would not be surprising if in this instance the soldiers were acting on his orders. Indeed, Pilate continued to maintain his position to the end: the whole thing was a purely internal affair among the Jews; let them take him, then, and crucify him (Jn 19:6).

At this point the high priests and their satellites, livid with rage, continued their fight with a perfect strategy, again shamelessly exploiting the ambiguity of Messianism and such terms as "Christ" and "Son of God." "We have a law," they replied, "and according to that law he ought to die, because he has claimed to be the Son of God" (Jn 19:7). Why, when Pilate heard this (Jn 19:8), did he become still more frightened? Was it, in this atmosphere of religiosity in a decadent empire, through fear of deicide? Such a hypothesis seems rather audacious. In fact, it is more simple and logical to assume that the Jewish leaders planned on Pilate's reaction but that after confirming his stubbornness in not wanting the trial to move out of the politicoreligious framework of Jewish Messianism, they outflanked the procurator from the far left by making him understand that in Jewish "orthodoxy" the Messiah, the Son of God, can indeed cause trouble for the Roman power, especially if the elite should join up with the Zealots. A few minutes later they made this quite specific by crying out, "If you set him free you are no friend of Caesar's; anyone who makes himself king is defying Caesar" (Jn 19:12). At this point the case had already been decided; the last ceremonial gesture ("Here is your king. Do you want me to crucify your king?"; Jn 19:14-15) was simply Pilate's final gesture of pride and obstinacy before surrendering to the typical fears of the high functionary. Those whom he governed only needed to repeat, "We have no king except Caesar" (*ibid.*) to clinch final victory for their cause.

In this way the Pharisees and some community leaders were once again shut up within their supposedly clever and supposedly patriotic opportunism, Pilate once again given reassurance regarding the loyalty of Jewish officials, and

Christ once and for all crucified. But the wrangling and ambiguity regarding the famous question of the royalty of Jesus continued—first, on the cross, with the title "the King of the Jews," in which Pilate found an outlet for his humiliated stubbornness and a recovery of the psychological victory that he had so much anticipated a little earlier (Lk 23:38; Mk 15:26; Mt 27:37; Jn 14:19–22); then, during his agony, during which both Jews and Roman soldiers, although with quite different attitudes and assumptions, spoke ironically about this madman, this grotesque and miserable fellow who pretended to be Christ, the Messiah, Son of God, and King of the Jews (Mk 15:32; Lk 23:35, 37; Mt 27:40, 42, 43).

Because the issue was of such importance to him (he died for it) and because the ambiguity of this political title of "king" had been so subtly turned against him, can it be that the accused, criminally executed, dead Jesus had given grounds for this action by his teaching? It is time to find out.

2

THE EXPLICIT POLITICAL
TEACHINGS OF JESUS

The Two Kingdoms

The teaching of Christ on the relationship of the two
realities that, according to circumstances, we distinguish or
reconcile into the binomials Church and world, spiritual
and temporal, Church and State—or formerly also into the
image of the two swords or of the throne and the altar—
was and remains both clear and tinged with that paradoxical or dialectical strain that runs through the whole of
evangelical thought.[1]

First, it was clear that Jesus was opposed to theocratic or
triumphant Messianism, by which the spiritual and the temporal would rest absolutely on the same foundation. We
need only be reminded, for example, that at the conclusion
of his first multiplication of the loaves, when tremendous
enthusiasm had been aroused among the crowd, "The people, seeing this sign that he had given, said 'This really is
the prophet who is to come into the world.' Jesus, who

[1] On the idea of paradox and Biblical upheaval, see again my
Quelle est donc cette Bonne Nouvelle? (1961), *passim.*

29

could see they were about to come and take him by force
and make him king, escaped back to the hills by himself"
(Jn 6:14–15).

From the point of view of the relationship between
throne and altar, Jesus' attitude toward taxation was, although fundamentally clear, more difficult to grasp at that
time. It is necessary to make a close study of the two major
scenes recorded on this subject, that of dues to be paid to
the temple (Mt 17:24–25) and that of tribute to be paid to
the Roman occupation authorities (Mk 12:13–17; Mt
22:15–22; Lk 20:20–26). They are very similar situations,
despite the divergence of the ultimate destination of the
fees, and this similarity is itself very instructive for us. In
effect, in both cases, the Lord resolved the problem, in an
atmosphere of lofty humor and indifference, with a kind of
sleight-of-hand performance, like a magician or public
entertainer. For the ten drachmas to the temple, there is the
"gag" of the fish caught by Peter at Jesus' command,
which held a shekel in his throat; [2] as regards paying
tribute to Rome, it was the trick question about the effigy
of Caesar. In both cases, the question is spontaneously
treated with disdain, with a supreme detachment. Jesus
condescends to pay, and we clearly see the watermark that
asks what all this matters to me. It is merely the domain of
the "world." At this first stage of analysis, we can only
conclude that there was what may well be called a kind of
indifferentism to temporal power and to its temporal manifestations in general.

But we cannot stop there, for there is at the same time an
important difference between these two incidents. In the
matter of imperial tribute, the Lord did not say whether or
not he is obedient to the law—neither yes nor no—all we

[2] The Attic statera (shekel) corresponded to the aureus of
Augustus and was the equivalent in weight (8 g. 60) of the Attic
didrachma of silver.

know is that the farce he has played with these malignant interlocutors simply ended with the tribute *in fact* being paid ("Render to Caesar that which is Caesar's"). On the contrary, in regard to the ten drachmas for the temple, Christ positively explained to Peter that he was not compliant:

"Simon, what is your opinion? From whom do the kings of the earth take toll or tribute? From their sons or from foreigners?" And when he replied, "From foreigners," Jesus said, "Well then the sons are exempt. However, so as not to offend these people, go to the lake and cast a hook; take the first fish that bites, open its mouth and there you will find a shekel; take it and give it to them for me and for you."

The radical freedom of Jesus in regard to this tax is underlined at the end of his explanation, which expresses the transcendence of the law (under which we were slaves, Saint Paul was to say) in the new alliance, and by the deliberately unusual and even exceptional result: in order not to scandalize the weak, Christ would pay but without really paying, because it would not be out of his pocket. It is a special derogation of the laws of nature; here Christ's intention is quite obvious, which settles the question.

There must be an explanation for this notable divergence. The reason for it appears simple enough: the evangelical reversal of the order of things does not immediately and directly involve the purely civil, purely temporal power, which remains what it was—a part of "the world." Its direct target, on the contrary, is the Law, that theocratic law that is both civil and religious and that the new Law wishes to complete, building on what is best in it, on what alone is genuinely alive, and transcending the rest. In the episode about paying tribute to Caesar, the fundamental point seems to be that there is no common measure between God and Caesar, between the Kingdom of God and the politicoeconomic structure. Therefore, settle your questions on taxation sensibly, but the essential question of your life is what you owe to God. Do not confuse these two things.

The significance of the text on the tithe in support of the temple is quite different. Ultimately, Christ was free in regard to this tax because the temple belonged to him; he was the son, not the slave, of the religious system. At the same time, from the viewpoint of a purely political analysis such as we are presenting here, he did not accept the assumption that a religious obligation should be transformed into the law of a political society. This is not an isolated incident. Jesus constantly rejected the legal validity of any moral and religious obligation to theocratic laws and customs—in other words, to any cementing together of the two kingdoms. Caesar distinguished between them; Jesus returned the emperor's insignia to him more or less disdainfully while implicitly recognizing the value of his law. The Pharisees did not distinguish between them; Jesus, even though in fact he complied with it, refused to give any value to their law, which, precisely because of this confusion of the two kingdoms, could no longer be the law of God.

This was a constant attitude of Jesus. In addition to raising questions about taxes, the Gospel shows him attacking and transgressing rabbinic interpretations of the Sabbath law, reminding his audience that it is the Son of Man, not the lawyers, who is the master of the Sabbath (Lk 6:5; Mk 2:27; Mt 12:8; Jn 5:16–17). Jesus also made clear that he opposed the law in Deuteronomy calling for the death penalty for adultery (Jn 8:3–11); he created a public disturbance by driving the money changers out of the temple (Lk 19:45–46; Mk 11:15–17; Mt 21:12–13; Jn 2:13–17). Consistently, therefore, every time he encountered a religious law that had been misappropriated by the spirit of civil law and thus drawn outside the great flow of divine love, Christ refused it. He did not want the two areas to be confused—what belongs to the world and what belongs to God, the temporal and the spiritual. Insistent that the latter not serve the former, he made a strong demand for the pre-eminence of the religious. That is also why, at the decisive final moment of his trial, he said to Pilate, and in this way almost excused him, "The one who handed me over to you has the greater guilt" (Jn 19:11). Pilate thus became a kind of secular arm who looked upon the defendant in front of him as a mystical agitator and found the problems he posed fundamentally wearisome, whereas Caiaphas, as we have seen, had traded abominably on the emotional overtones of the phrase "King of the Jews," had been dishonest, and had constantly and cleverly mixed the registers of the temporal and the spiritual, sacrilegiously confusing the frontiers of the two kingdoms.

Our Lord, on the other hand, carefully and formally distinguished between these two kingdoms. This is seen, first, in his famous answer to the Pharisees in connection with the question of giving tribute: "Give back to Caesar what belongs to Caesar—and to God what belongs to God" (Mk 12:17; Lk 20:25; Mt 22:21) and especially in the great text that presents his tranquil conversation with Pilate at the last moments of his trial. After admitting that he is indeed the King of the Jews, Jesus went on to clarify what he meant: "Mine is not a kingdom of this world; if my kingdom were of this world, my men would have fought to prevent my being surrendered to the Jews. But my kingdom is not of this kind. . . . Yes, I am a king. I was born for this, I came into the world for this: to bear witness to the truth; and all who are on the side of truth listen to my voice" (Jn 18:36–37). The specific Kingdom of Christ, therefore, is completely spiritual and interior although visible and social; it represents the truth that delivers us, in which political force has no part.

But in the face of this power, or alongside or beneath it, Jesus recognized that another power exists, another kingdom. To the procurator, who reproached him for not trying to defend himself—"Surely you know that I have power to release you and I have power to crucify you?"—he replied, "You would have no power over me if it had not been given you from above; that is why the one who handed me over to you has the greater guilt" (Jn 19:10–11). The world, therefore, to the degree it has a power holds that power from God. This kingdom of the world, consequently, is not completely bad or totally nonexistent; it has a certain "consistency." The sin of the one who makes a foolish use of that power or acts inopportunely is less serious than the sin of the man who makes use of the spiritual as if it is a temporal power and of the temporal as if it is a spiritual power.

What we must hold on to here is that the two kingdoms are distinct; that one is superior to the other and, indeed, alone is necessary ("Seek first the Kingdom of God and his justice, and the rest shall be added to you"); and that it is a sacrilege to mix them. In a later section, we must examine the relationships that exist between these two kingdoms.

Evangelical Political Consciousness

But first, it is necessary for us to take seriously the following question: is it true that the "Kingdom of Heaven" is disincarnate and hovers about in an atmosphere where economics and politics have no meaning?

Nothing could be farther from the truth. Moreover, such a thing is immediately improbable in view of what we have already seen of how profoundly rooted Jesus and his evangelical revelation were in economic and political soil. As far as the teaching itself is concerned, we can already ascertain, for example, that of some two hundred parables, major and minor, more than a third are taken up with scenes or elements of political life (family, profession, society) and that of the thirty-five major parables almost all are "political." It is not irrelevant to our subject that, in order to preach the Kingdom of God, Jesus made use of the history of the earthly city and of the world. In this way he called to mind family life—with stories of the prodigal son, the two sons, the bridegroom, childbirth, the sullen children, the father and his child, the women grinding grain; professional life—with references to the shepherd, the unfaithful treasurer, the faithful steward and the unfaithful servant, the workers in the vineyard, the murderous winegrowers, the sower, the shepherd who is attacked, the blind guide, the doctor, the pastor, the fishermen, the publican; economic life—with all the parables of professional life as well as the story of the lost drachma, the mines and the talents (in which banking activity is mentioned), the precious pearl, the purses, the eye of a needle, Lazarus and the rich man, the gift made to the rich, the watchful landlord, the new suit, the treasury. All in all, social and political life [3] is sketched out in the parables that we have mentioned, as well as in those about the troublesome friend, war, the discourteous guests, the wicked judge, the master of the house, the Pharisee and the publican, the wedding garment, the good Samaritan, the tower, the bandit who is driven out, the sword, the son and the slave, the priests of the temple, princes, the reception of a lodger, reconciliation before trial, a levy, the divided kingdom, the Sanhedrin,

[3] When it is convenient and sufficiently clear in context, we may sometimes use the words "social" and "political" in the current and restricted sense. It remains well understood that, in any strict analysis, the social is an aspect of political reality that covers everything related to the social being of man (including economics).

obedient servants, vigilant attendants and those who consider themselves useless, respectful soldiers, the tribunal, thrones . . .[4]

Political teaching—in the sense we are using the term "politics" in this essay—is obvious. But was politics given positive value for itself, or was it explicitly opposed by Christ? Did Jesus look on politics as an objective of his action? Did he want to transform it? After all, the most disincarnate of spiritual leaders draws his language and examples from the concrete social context in which he lives. Of itself, this does not mean that he has any intention of acting on it. Did Jesus explicitly have the intention of transforming this material, and if so, in what sense and in what manner? The question needs to be clarified.

In fact, the parables are immediately teeming with a spiritual meaning, because they teach us about the Kingdom of God. "My kingdom is not of this world." It should by now be established that the substance of this Kingdom, its reality, its structures, even its very name, are expressed in terms modeled on a reality, a substance and a structure that is political, and refer to them. Besides, the entry into this Kingdom involves a kind of behavior toward political realities, including economics, justice, and social relationships. Political realities not only are images to express the Kingdom of God but are related, by means of the teaching of Jesus, to that spiritual reality that is the Kingdom. In this sense, it is necessary for us to ask ourselves to what degree the Gospel includes an explicit political teaching and in what degree the Kingdom of Heaven itself has a political value.

[4] We are not giving the scriptural references for the parables that are here being classified; it would be pointless and pedantic to do so. What we are concerned with here does not have any directly instructional value in the domain of politics. Besides, it is easy enough to locate these parables through the use of any standard concordance.

Poverty and Money

There is, in fact, no lack of positive political teaching (or direct political implications of spiritual teaching) in which Jesus does not separate—have we paid enough attention to this? We shall have the occasion to return to it more systematically at the end of our analysis—the *law* of the Kingdom of God from earthly *law*. Does he even distinguish between them? It is not at all obvious.

Without by any means allowing ourselves to become confined within a Marxist framework, let us begin our inventory of political consciousness on the economic level. In order not to get lost in detail and to get right down to essentials, we can say that the whole moral teaching of the Gospel in regard to economics is structured by a tension between *poverty* and *money*. Poverty and Jesus are placed on the positive pole; wealth, money, and the world as it is are on the negative side.

Poverty, and even the destitution in which Jesus asked us to recognize his own countenance, is seen in positive terms: "For I was hungry and you gave me food; I was thirsty and you gave me drink; I was a stranger and you made me welcome; naked and you clothed me, sick and you visited me, in prison and you came to see me. . . . I tell you solemnly, in so far as you did this to one of the least of these brothers of mine, you did it to me" (Mt 25:35–40). Certainly, in this great text we are dealing with an evocation of the Last Judgment, the threshold of the Kingdom "prepared for you since the foundation of the world" (Mt 25:34), of the Kingdom of God that has reached its term of maturity. Nevertheless, the actions endorsed by this judgment certainly refer to earthly existence, and it is very much a question of real hunger, thirst, poverty, and human misery—and not simply symbolic or spiritual conditions.

In the same way, the poor people whom Christ asked us to invite are real, because they are unable to return the invitation (Lk 14:13). The extreme poverty of the Lord, who did not even have a place to rest his head (Lk 9:58; Mt 8:20), was equally real; so were the instructions given to *all* (the pericope is not situated within a context of the counsels) to sell what we have and give what is received as alms (Lk 12:33). It is not astonishing, therefore, that the evangelical teaching of the Beatitudes starts off with the call to poverty. Of course, it is a matter of being poor "in spirit" (Mt 5:3), but this does not mean a symbolic or purely spiritual poverty; besides, does not Luke simply write, "How happy are you who are poor" (Lk 6:20)? Poverty of spirit is invoked, it would seem, because it has a moral suggestion and a religious value, referring to something that is not simply endured but is also willed, directed, and made use of. Besides, how could we imagine that we could escape with a purely mental poverty when Jesus imperatively ordered those who wished to follow him completely no longer to possess anything (Lk 18:18 ff.; Mk 10:17 ff.; Mt 19:16 ff.) and strongly recommended that everyone do the same: "Do not store up treasures for yourself on earth, where moths and woodworms destroy them . . ." (Mt 6:20; Lk 12:33)? The Gospel is truly a morality of poor men, as much as that of sinners.

At the negative pole, on the other hand, are the rich and money, both stigmatized with such a positive realism and clarity that here again any possibility of a purely mystical, spiritual, or mental interpretation is completely excluded. The parable of the faithless steward (Lk 16) presents two conclusions, but, although it is hard to say why, we seem generally to retain only the first. This itself seems quite relevant, because it puts money in the role of a rather low instrument of the one thing necessary. The second conclusion, however, is even more curious because of the implications it contains regarding distributive justice, of which we shall speak again, and also because it repeats, in order that this be well understood, the epithet "tainted" (or "dishonest") in regard to money. Money is tainted, money is dishonest; as the note in the Jerusalem Bible says, "Money is here called tainted not only because its owner is here presumed to have gained it dishonestly but because great wealth is rarely acquired without sharp practice." We shall not hesitate to go further: from the context, it seems that we are dealing here with a true Homeric epithet presented as an absolute, not simply a reference to the mode of acquisition. Whatever the case may be, moreover, Luke (16:13) links this great text to the decisive conclusion: "No servant can be the slave of two masters. . . . You cannot be the slave both of God and of money" (see Mt 6:24). In other words, there is a radical antinomy between these two poles. And money here means real money, not an image, a representation, the idea of money, or attachment to money; no, it is simply money.

We must here explain precisely what money was in the socioeconomic context of Palestine in the days of Christ; we must at the same time indicate what it signified in language and psychology in order to grasp better what Jesus was personifying by his use of the term. In the area where Christ grew up the economy was rural and underdeveloped, and it would seem that the Mammon of precious metals was, first of all, the symbol of nonproductive stockpiling and of the feeling of power. In any case, what Jesus was especially attacking was the domination of money in social relations, the place that it held in the life of men. Man himself was projected in his money; if he received security and a sense of sufficiency; through money he assessed his own value, and it became his norm of life and judgment. The poor were simply those who had no money.

But has all this changed very much since the time of Christ, even though money is no longer hoarded in one's home but is invested in the economy? Does not modern man judge himself as well as others in terms of income and bank account? Are not profit and wealth the primary attachments that prevent man from being free to pursue life in the spirit of the Gospel? Are they not the gateway to injustice? Indeed, are they anything but idols?

When profit makers were installed in the temple, Jesus adopted a violent attitude. During one of his rare displays of holy anger, he drove out the sellers (Lk 19:45-46; Mk 11:15-17; Jn 2:13-17). The "den of thieves" is a more violent epithet than "tainted" or "dishonest" money. When profit making was established in the temple, every mercantile transaction became a depredation. To allow Mammon, the idol par excellence, to be implanted in the temple was truly a sacrilege.

This pessimistic attitude of Christ to money is perhaps most painfully expressed in his famous comparison: "Yes, it is easier for a camel to pass through the eye of a needle than for a rich man to enter the kingdom of God" (Lk 18:25; Mk 10:25; Mt 19:24) or in this other saying: "But alas for you who are rich: you are having your consolation now" (Lk 6:24). Is it simply a question of ill-gotten wealth or were not Christ's words more severe? Was he not directly attacking wealth itself? Was not money itself being cursed?

We have still another indication of the importance of the subject in Jesus' mind: of all the realities the Lord made use of in his parables to signify something, wealth—money —is the only one that does not mean anything but itself. For example, in the parables of Lazarus (Lk 16:19-31) and of the rich man (Lk 12:16-21), wealth has no second meaning; [5] it is simply that which is directly in opposition to the Kingdom of Heaven.

The Evasion of Economic Reality

Looked at again in the harsh or "economic" light of the evangelical proclamation, we begin to see the harm done by a certain "spiritual" interpretation—which, of course, has nothing in common with the pneumatic exegesis of some of the Fathers? We shall deal with this briefly now, but it would also be true with regard to each of the points that we are going to touch on in what follows.

"Happy are the poor and accursed are the rich," the Lord has said. With the help of many nuances and considerable softening of emphasis, are we not able immediately to reassure the rich, allowing them to think that Jesus was only talking about a few exceptionally rare cases of wicked rich men? The bank accounts and preferred shares of stock, the servants, the limousines, the lavish vacations, the abundance of jewelry, the preoccupation with profit and money—all this has very little importance if one is detached from it. But if someone is so detached, however, why would he possess it? We even end up talking about the parable of Lazarus and the *bad* rich man, although there is nothing in Luke's text to justify this epithet—he simply said "a rich man." Perhaps a review of this question is overdue. Is it enough to give to charities, or even to set up clinics and recreation centers for the poor, and to have an upright intention in order to avoid the curse of wealth? We need to take this up again with a great deal of vigor

[5] It is remarkable that in the case of precious metals the evangelical context always indicates very clearly (see, for example, the parables of the pearl and of the lost drachma) if, in a special instance, the precious object is understood in a purely spiritual sense, by contrast with the many passages in which money is taken and judged simply as pure economic reality.

and perhaps identify what constitutes wealth in our day
and age and the source of its contradiction with the Gospel.
It would surely be a serious matter to falsify the Gospel by
using deception. Those who rest comfortably about this
too easily should be reminded that it is possible that they
are bad shepherds. For Christ has not said, "Cursed be the
rich who are wicked." And the reason for this, as presented
both in the pericope of the Beatitudes and in the parable of
Lazarus, is quite interesting: the rich have received their
consolation already here on earth; therefore they will have
no part in the Kingdom. Nor did Jesus say that under certain conditions the rich could be saved; on the contrary, he
stated that it was practically impossible for them to work
out their salvation. And he was not speaking of being rich
in spirit but purely and simply of being rich—of having
material, economic, and hence political wealth.

In the face of this, all sorts of reactions are possible while
maintaining intellectual honesty as well as logic—if not
orthodoxy. One might say, for example, that the Gospel
teaching is stupid or impossible or that it makes us angry or
that we can admire it without imitating it—or even that the
Gospel should be handled with caution and that the
Church has made necessary compromises with it.

Only one reaction is dishonest and illogical: pretending
that Jesus said what he did not say.

Let us beware of assuming too easily that the Lord and
those who listened to him were not aware of the paradoxical
character of this teaching on money and wealth and of its
apparently utopian character. Certainly, the small and decisive parable of the camel and the eye of a needle is an
image, but it serves to highlight the subversive character of
this teaching; Christ's hearers were not deceived, as is de-
monstrated by their immediate reaction, as noted by the
evangelist: "They were more astonished than ever. 'In that
case,' they said to one another, 'who can be saved?' Jesus

gazed at them. 'For men,' he said, 'it is impossible, but not for God: because everything is possible for God.' " (Mk 10:26–27; Mt 19:25–26; Lk 18:26–27). An economist could say, it is true, that his science does not permit him to depend on God in this fashion, but that is another story, about which we shall have the occasion to speak again. First, however, let us at least retain this much: no matter how religious the essence of Jesus' teaching on poverty is, it nevertheless becomes incarnate here economically and it is a condemnation of wealth.

The Evangelical Potlatch

Certain communist commentators have tried to find the traces of capitalism even in the Gospel, at least in that of Saint Luke. They had in mind especially the way Christ treated the question of wages in parables like that of the workers sent into the vineyard (Mt 20:1–16) and that of the talents and the pounds (Mt 25:14–30; Lk 19:11–27). Our impression, however, is that the Gospel hardly touches on the question of salaries. The parables in question appear to us primarily as pure images intended to bring men closer to the supernatural and paradoxical reality of the Kingdom of God in its most theological substance.

In our opinion, the Gospel's indifference to salaries would even be explainable in the most logical terms: from the moment that Jesus condemns money, the problem of salaries is no longer of interest to him.

At the most, we could say with some likelihood that in a world in which social relationships were mainly based on money—and from that point of view, are not such relationships in contradiction with the Bible?—these two parables, by analogical transposition, can have a certain exemplary value in leading us toward a realization that would be more in keeping with the evangelical ideal.

From this point of view, it becomes interesting to note that the two stories end with two apparently contradictory "morals": in the case of the talents, retribution is as proportional to the labor expended as it is inversely proportional to needs; he who already possesses the most and who has made the greatest effort is also given the most in addition. The story of the workers in the vineyard, on the contrary, extols a special kind of goodness that, going much further than justice, recovers a kind of superjustice that correlates both need and consideration. Those who have worked only a short time receive just as much as those who have borne "the burden of the day and the heat"; in relative value, therefore, they are receiving a great deal more. But it is easy enough to conjecture, from indications in the text, that they are being paid in this way not only because of their basic needs, which are equal to those of their colleagues (this is the purpose of the equality in wages in absolute value), but also because of the humiliation and agony experienced by men who had been left on the shelf and were idle against their will (this is the reason for their better treatment in terms of relative value). In sum, for the purpose of brevity and in order to schematize, we could say that the parables of the talents and the pounds have a "liberal capitalist" economic basis, whereas the parable of the workers in the vineyard suggests a "socialist" style. To support such a typology, there is even an appropriate general atmosphere: the stories of the talents and the pounds take place in the framework of the money market and banking; the workers in the vineyard spend their day in the milieu of the agricultural proletariat.

We are reminded that the Gospel does not offer any direct teaching on wages, so it is difficult to draw a neat conclusion. Nevertheless, it still seems possible to suggest that to the degree that one wanted to find by transposition some suggestions on this subject, no encouragement is given that attitude that takes refuge in a transcendent indifferentism—as was the case in regard to the earthly kingdom. In fact, from the strictly economic point of view —if one puts the spiritual meaning of their gestures in parentheses—the behavior of the master of the vineyard is infinitely more in keeping with the evangelical spirit than that of "the man of noble origin," because he is expressing an economy of perfect love.

Just as this perfect love implies a contempt for money and ignorance regarding wages, it leads naturally to an economics based on gift, which we could call an evangelical potlatch [6] and which is expressed in the commandment "Give to everyone who asks you, and do not ask for your property back from the man who robs you" (Lk 6:30; Mt 5:42). This little principle, we can see clearly, is important by reason of its meaning and implications because, in addition to the economy of gratuitous exchange it indicates, a radical limitation of the right to property is quite clearly implied. This takes on greater importance when we have recognized that this teaching is not situated as part of the presentation of what are called the "evangelical counsels"; we are here dealing with a precept, one of those that arise from the fact that Christ brought the law to fulfillment. Besides, there can be no question of making this precept disappear in a spiritual and symbolic interpretation. All the precepts in this area of Jesus' teaching are completely social in the material sense of the term, having to do with improv-

[6] The reader unfamiliar with the works of social anthropology might profitably consult, in the absence of the important thesis of G. Davy, the perceptive essay of Marcel Mauss *Le Don*, reprinted in *Sociologie et Anthropologie* (1950), pp. 145–279. Potlach, a kind of economy practiced by certain archaic tribes, ignores money and contracts and consists, by a sort of tacit "gentleman's agreement," in a constant exchange of gifts. Obviously we are using the term here by analogy, for the rules of potlach are in fact quite complicated.

ing men's attitudes toward homicide, adultery, the repudiation of one's wife, vows, the treatment of enemies, and so on. Moreover, in this particular situation, we even have a proof *a contrario* there exists another passage in the Gospel (Lk 11:5–13; Mt 7:7–11) in which the gift and the loan are utilized by Christ in parables (the troublesome friend) of the prayer to the Father in Heaven. This is not absolutely the case of Luke 6:30 and Matthew 5:42. Let us recall, finally, that the evangelical gift should be bestowed with delicacy, "in secret" (Mt 6:2–4).

In saying that Luke 6:30 is a precept and not a simple counsel, we are not unaware that we are concerned primarily with a law of behavior in the area of justice. Christ is giving men a new way of looking at the subject of property, a new way of thinking about socioeconomic relationships. According to it, worrying about defending our rights and privileges, even when they are endangered, can never be our first order of business—such a concern would only reveal alienation and a lack of love. Jesus demanded a terrible detachment from men in regard to their rights, a detachment that is not simply symbolic and intentional but is to be translated into real, concrete situations in the manner suggested by Luke 6:30.

The Primacy of the Kingdom

We cannot terminate an analysis of the economic teaching of the Gospel without meditating on the magnificent text on the lilies of the field and the birds of the air (Lk 12:22, 31; Mt 6:25–34). What did Christ tell us? Was he insisting that we should not busy ourselves with the world of economics, represented in this instance by food and clothing? Not at all. But he was telling us not to be *anxious* about it, because "the soul is more than food and the body is more than clothing." It is up to the pagans, and to those who cling to "the world," to worry constantly about these things: "The nations of the world are strong in their pursuit of all this." This ought not to be the case for the children of the Kingdom: "Your father knows that you have need of all that. But seek first the Kingdom of Heaven and all that will be given to you in addition."

This idea, that economic needs would be filled "in addition," holds an important place in the evangelical doctrine not only of economics but also of the whole realm of politics and in regard to all the problems we are taking up in this book. We Christians are forewarned—and through us, others (materialists, capitalists, and socialists) may hear the same warning—that a preoccupation with material abundance alone could not govern either a life or a civilization but would only strengthen the forces of injustice and egoism. Everything that builds up the Kingdom of God takes precedence over the economic objectives that a civilization or an individual may give themselves. Relationships among men and our basic attitudes to life ought to be directed to God and the laws of His Kingdom. In this way, both what is necessary and what is essential in practice is assured at the same time. The rule of success for an economy that would be truly worthy of man is provided by the point of view that accepts the primacy of God's Kingdom and the subordination of the rest to what the Kingdom implies. If it is true that the Lord is the only Lord and that he has revealed the truth to us, how could it be that what he has asked us to do in the domain of economics would not be the truth? Should we not begin to understand, therefore, that if our world today is sick and dying, if it fails even the economic and political tasks about which it is so very anxious and that seem to be the object of *all* its care, this is precisely to the degree that men are not seeking first the Kingdom of God and we Christians seem incapable of giving them the desire to seek for it?

3

THE SOCIAL AND THE
POLITICAL

At the frontier of economics and what is commonly called politics, the area we often refer to as the social extends to the very horizon of the political universe of the Gospel. Think, for example, of the place that the evangelists gave to children and to the sick, upon whom the solicitude of the Savior constantly descended; we have already referred to the emphasis on woman in the Gospel. It is true that the miracles of curing had an essentially spiritual, Messianic significance. Nevertheless, the pity of the Lord for the wretched and afflicted was frequently in evidence; he showed pity for the crowd that was hungry and for the sorrow of Martha and Mary and the widow of Naim. It can be said that, notwithstanding their value as supernatural signs, on the human level the miracles were also the sign of a heart full of pity and the effect of a work of assistance to a humanity that is destitute to the degree that those who bear responsibility for men do not accept it.

The Origin of Power

One of the great texts of the trial of Jesus, which we have analyzed in regard to the problem of the two powers, the spiritual and the temporal, also contains a passage (Jn 19:11) that determines the question of the origin of temporal power. Just after Pilate said to Jesus, "Surely you know I have power to release you and I have power to crucify you?" the latter replied, "You would have no power over me if it had not been given you from above. . . ."

Temporal power, therefore, is accorded by divine permission, but we also notice that there is no attempt to determine the mode of this delegation and the type of power. It is power as such; at the time of Jesus it was authoritarian, but the same principle would have been true if the power had been democratic. Such an approach only serves to reenforce what we have called, in connection with the political life of Jesus and the question of the two kingdoms, the political indifferentism of the Gospel at the formal level.[1]

There is a similar restraint about laying down specific rules when the idea of taxation is considered, no longer as the sign of the Gospel's thought on the two powers but in itself. John the Baptist, preparing the way for Christ, had simply reminded the tax gatherers of a few precepts of simple honesty, which have, nevertheless, the honor of being included in the evangelical collection; for example, "Exact no more than your rate" (Lk 3:13). Jesus, taking up the problem from the other side, that of the tax payer, spoke out plainly in the two great texts already cited, those having to do with the contribution for the temple and the coin

---

[1] On the precise meaning of this term, see pp. 80 ff.

for Caesar. If we look at his statements, no longer in terms of the two powers but in regard to the very question of taxation, we see that Jesus, in spite of the somewhat enigmatic character of his words, ordered us to submit to it, although not without a trace of lofty condescension because it is a question of money, a "worldly" problem.

Problems of Legal Justice: Theft, Homicide, Divorce, Oaths, Vengeance, Punishment, Judgment

In regard to problems of legal justice and common law the evangelical doctrine is quite precise, even in material detail. Robbery is denounced, even (which is not often mentioned) in the parable of the unfaithful steward. Although money, as we have seen, is considered "vile" and "unjust," it is necessary to be "faithful" to it—which means, in the context, not to steal it: "If then you cannot be trusted with money, that tainted thing, who will trust you with genuine riches? And if you cannot be trusted with what is not yours, who will give you what is your very own?" (Lk 16:11–12).[2]

The Mosaic prescription against homocide is recalled and even strengthened—or at least refined; anger and insult are forbidden as leading to murder, and immediate reconciliation is prescribed (Mt 5:21–23).

We see the same pattern in the evangelical teaching on adultery and divorce: evil desire, the repudiation of one's spouse, and marriage with a divorced partner are assimilated with adultery and condemned along with it (Mt 5:27–32; Lk 76:18; Jn 7:3–12, and elsewhere; Mk

---

[2] This point does not absurdly contradict the first "moral" (Lk 16:9), in which the steward is praised for making friends with "vile" money; he is praised for having subordinated money to more important goods, not for having made it dishonestly.

10:2–11; Mt 19:3–12, where monogamy is firmly established in absolute terms). Against some criticisms, Christ also reestablishes in its original purity and its absolute value the duty to give assistance to one's parents (Mk 7:10–13; Mt 15:4–6).

Every oath is forbidden, whether "secular" (swearing on one's head) or religious (swearing in the name of Heaven, the Throne of God, and so on). "All you need say is 'Yes' if you mean yes, 'No' if you mean no; anything more than this comes from the evil one" (Mt 5:33–37).

Besides, in a general way all assaults on what nowadays is called good morals and the general public good are forbidden: "fornication, theft, murder, adultery, avarice, deceit, indecency, envy, slander, pride, folly" (Mk 7:21–22; Mt 15:19). Nor should we lose sight of the fact that the Mosaic law in its entirety is not abrogated but completed. That is, what was positive in it is more clearly and profoundly revealed, but what it contained or had acquired that had grown hard or become formalistic was thrown as chaff into the fire of love.

Nevertheless, if all these prescriptions, which to begin with, have moral value (but moral values exist as such in action only to the degree that they govern concrete lives), are extremely firm, strict, and precise, punishment for their infringement is expressly reserved to justice of God. First of all, the law of retaliation is abolished and even replaced by its exact opposite: ". . . if anyone hits you on the right cheek, offer him the other as well; if a man takes you to law and would have your tunic, let him have your cloak as well" (Mt 5:38–40). But Christ went a great deal further: he has even forbidden us to condemn or judge anyone except ourselves; it is up to each of us, while removing the mote from our own eye, to improve the world and advance the Kingdom: "Do not judge, and you will not be judged

yourselves; do not condemn, and you will not be condemned
yourselves; grant pardon, and you will be pardoned"
(Lk 6:37–42; Mt 7:1–5).

We must indeed ask ourselves if all this is simply a matter
of a vague attitude or if Christ does not intend it to be applied even in the juridical and legal domain. Surely, its application is complicated, but we cannot avoid the question
by too easily establishing a split between a morality intended for purely internal and spiritual usage and another
that would have repercussions in the practical conduct of
life and in the organization of social and political structures.

The episode of the adulterous woman should put us on
guard against too spiritual an exegesis. Certainly the point
of the text is the revelation of the mercy of God beyond all
human judgment, for the drama does not take place simply
in the world of ideas or even in terms of parable but is
played out within a concrete, lived situation. The woman is
dragged before a court; the scribes and Pharisees invoke the
law of Moses in order to justify stoning her. This law,
however religious in essence, possessed the validity of civil
law in the Judaic Theocracy as was true of all laws and
regulations, both civil and religious). It was, therefore, a
kind of contemporary court session, which we are able to
observe. This was the trial Jesus forbade; let that one of
you who is without sin throw the first stone. Jesus snatched
this woman from the judgment of men and denied to the
court its competence to judge. We all know the sequel,
both astonishing and admirable. Let us not forget, however, that the offense itself was not denied or ignored;
the last word was "Go, sin no more." But the order not to
judge delinquents and not to condemn them was here applied to a real-life situation; it was applied not only to the
interior (religious) tribunal but to the exterior (civil) tribunal, because the woman's life was saved. Does this example only refer to an individual case? Was Jesus simply

protesting that the acts of religious law and conscience should not replace the courts of law, which can condemn in terms of civil justice? Or are we dealing with a more radical command not to judge wrongdoers? Was Christ systematically rejecting all punishment that might be meted out by the civil tribunal, or did he simply think that in this particular case the punishment, along with the legislation that calls for it, was excessive? Was his opposition based on the consideration that questions of this kind should not be punished by coercion or death? According to Matthew, the only punishment of the Church tribunal is excommunication. There is a whole ensemble of questions which need to be studied here; it is impossible not to come to more precise conclusions.

The Weekly Rest

The Sabbath rest involves another set of laws that concern the civil legislator and the citizen as well as the priest and believer. If the evangelical teaching is looked at from the purely political point of view, we recognize that, according to the mind of Jesus, the Sabbath cannot be invoked against a work of urgent necessity, like satisfying hunger (recall the episode in which the disciples picked corn on the Sabbath: Lk 6:1–5; Mk 2:23–28; Mt 19:1–8) or curing the crippled woman (Lk 13:10–17), the sick man at the pool of Bethesda (Jn 5:1–17), and the man with dropsy (Lk 14:–16). In a general way, the golden rule for the juridical interpretation of the problems regarding the Sabbath was expressed during the incident when the Pharisees were scandalized because Jesus' disciples were picking and eating corn as they went along: "The sabbath was made for man, not man for the Sabbath" (Mk 2:27).

Peace and Nonviolence

What political problem is more human and more agonizing than war?

On this subject, as in the matter of taxes, when soldiers in his audience asked what they should do, John the Baptist had limited himself to reminding them of traditional principles of good humanist morality—which already presume, as men of our time know all too well, a rarely attained level of perfection: "No intimidation! No extortion! Be content with your pay" (Lk 3:14). What army, however, or what police force, either before or after the Gospel, has been or is free of violence, plunder, and brutality?

However this may be, the specifically evangelical Revelation, as received from the mouth of the Lord, is infinitely more radical and once again calls for a true revolution. Not only should the disciples of Christ be "in peace with another" (Mk 9:50), but such a condition constitutes their very definition: "Happy the peacemakers: they shall be called the sons of God" (Mk 5:9). It follows from this that all recourse to force and violence is absolutely proscribed: "But I say this to you: offer the wicked man no resistance. On the contrary, if anyone hits you on the right cheek, offer him the other as well . . ." (Mt 5:39). We might remind ourselves of the extent to which these laws were observed by Christ himself during the course of his arrest and trial and execution. As Jesus said to Peter in the Garden of Gethsemane, "Put your sword back, for all who draw the sword will die by the sword" (Mt 26:52); his bearing and every gesture manifested sweetness, peace, and pardon in the face of violence and passion.

Certainly the behavior of Christ before the high court can be explained also by other reasons. The Messiah was to be—and wished to be—handed over to his enemies. The salvific necessity of Christ's death is too well anchored to the Gospel for us to forget it. Certainly, too, this trial was no ordinary trial; it was the epilogue of a religious mission that Christ's enemies tried, with bad faith, to turn into a crime. Nevertheless, is not the Lord's behavior in the course of this trial an example of a much broader significance for every accused man? The question deserves close examination.

Indeed, it forces us to confront a debate very much alive today. Have we succeeded in getting a clear picture on which to base our attitude toward those who attempt to practice active nonviolence in our times? How much do we understand of these men who try to give testimony and act as Christians in the most painful political conflicts? Yet it is incontestable that nonviolence is a direct and immediate consequence of the evangelical law. We ought to ask ourselves if its validity extends to only a few individual cases or if it has meaning and evangelical justification even in the political arena, even in the matter of the defense plans that nations are constantly drawing up. Physical violence is only a caricature of real force; the Christian ought to be capable of undergoing it without adopting it, of assuming it without making use of it, of having a sword without availing oneself of it. Is it not surprising that such a vision of things, which is so close to the Gospel, has suddenly been recalled to us by men who are outside the Christian tradition, who would strenuously resist the suggestion that they are Christians? It may well be that this young and vigorous growth is springing up today in the fields of the Church because it has profited from the fertilizer imported from the banks of the Ganges; nevertheless, it is truly a sprout that has come from the Gospel.

Loving One's Enemies

Nonviolence is better explained and takes on its full meaning in the climate of total love, the universal wave of

charity that encompasses God and men and impregnates all
of evangelical doctrine. This commandment is truly the
kernel of the new law, the first commandment (Lk
10:25–28; Mk 12:28–34; Mt 22:34–40), the new commandment (Jn 13:34). Here again, it is not a question of
avoiding practical implications by rhapsodizing about a
completely spiritual love; the love commanded by the
Gospel is an effective love that would inform the whole of
social life, and it is according to this standard that we will
be judged on the last day: "I was hungry and you gave me
food; I was thirsty and you gave me drink; I was a stranger
and you made me welcome; naked and you clothed me;
sick and you visited me; in prison and you came to see me"
(Mt 25:34–36).

This love is universal and is even able to encompass enemies (Lk 6:27–36; Mt 5:43–48); indeed, it extends to the
point that the idea of enemy is almost suppressed. This is
the fundamental meaning of the cure of the Samaritan leper
(Lk 17:12–19) because, as we know, the Samaritans were
the intimate enemies of the Jews of Judea and Galilee. The
point is even more obvious in the parable of the Good Samaritan (Lk 10:30–37), which at the same time establishes
the definition of neighbor because it was narrated as an answer to the precise question, posed by a scribe, "Who is my
neighbor?" Most commentaries on the story do not pay
sufficient attention to its ending, where Christ asked,
"Which of these three, do you think, proved himself a
neighbor to the man who fell into the brigands' hands?"
and the doctor of the law responded, "The one who took
pity on him." This grammatical reversal is full of meaning;
it is not the wounded man who was the neighbor but the
Samaritan who became the neighbor of the wounded man
by drawing near to him. The neighbor, finally, is the one
who is close at hand and, as a consequence, the one with
whom we get close. This is the commandment of universal

love, which we understand perfectly when, without any contradiction, it reaches out to our enemies as much as, or even more than, to our friends precisely because both they and we have greater need of drawing together.

It is useless to underline further to what extent the application of this doctrine of the love of neighbor and of one's "enemies" is intended by Christ to be the anchor of social realities.

Universal love has, therefore, important implications in regard to a man's attitude to his country. Surely, the Lord was no more exempt from an attachment to the land of his birth than he was to the sweetness and the sorrow of carnal friendship; nothing in the tenor of the incident in which he shed tears over the city of Jerusalem (Lk 19:41–44) would allow us to doubt it, to the profit of a purely mystical interpretation. Preachers who are desperate for scripture references for a sermon on Saint Joan of Arc or for any patriotic holiday and who utilized the beautiful passage in which Jesus wept for Jerusalem in order to justify all sorts of patriotic excesses should also take into consideration the general silence of the Gospel on the subject of war —which in itself is significant—as well as some rare but formal pericopes that point to as nonnationalistic a doctrine as possible. First, there is the incident of the synagogue at Nazareth (Lk 4:22–30; Mk 6:1–6; Mt 13:54–58; Jn 4:44), the moral of which was summed up by Christ when he said that "no prophet is held in honor in his own country," and by his narration of the story of Elijah's being sent not to his own country but to Zarepath, a Sidonian town, and the story of Elisha's curing not the lepers of Israel but the Syrian Naaman. In order to grasp fully the force of this text, it is indispensable to forget its cut-rate version as a somewhat silly proverb ("No one is a prophet in his own country") and take into account the very clear indication that the notions of fatherland and Kingdom of God share little that is compatible, because the latter ignores any nationalistic consideration and implies (see Elisha and Elijah) a total openness to all countries.

Certainly the opposition expressed by Christ is not directly between one's country and the universal but between an unfaithful chosen people and the universal people of God. But this has its repercussions on the very idea of fatherland, because it offers a new vision of man and of humanity in the design of God.

The same indication, moreover, is furnished by major texts dealing with fathers, mothers, and brothers and sisters, which have a direct bearing on our problem of fatherland when we realize that, both for etymology and for everyday reality, the fatherland is the place to which one is rooted by blood: "My mother and my brothers are those who hear the word of God and put it into practice" (Lk 8:19–21; Mk 3:31–36; Mt 12:46–50).

All this is clearly full of a negation of any frontier imposed by particularisms, and there is no point in emphasizing, in order to lessen its practical implications, that we are dealing here with the law of the Kingdom of God. After all, each disciple of Christ is imperiously summoned to do all that he can to hasten the coming of that very Kingdom. It will surely not come if its rules are not followed in practice; on the contrary, what is required is that we follow in their direction with a love without frontiers.

But this love is also a force of liberty, precisely because it detaches us from all that is not true.[3] The old order of the slavery of law is overturned; we are adopted sons following the rule of the new alliance, the new testament. It is in this context that Christ's attitude toward the rent to be paid to the temple can be understood. "Children are free," he said,

[3] "If you make my word your home you will indeed be my disciples, you will learn the truth and the truth will make you free" (Jn 8:31–32).

not with the freedom of anarchy, but in terms of another, rediscovered law (that of total love) that, inscribing itself also in rituals and regulations, will nevertheless never allow itself to become withered and evaporate into ritualism. It is not a "morality without obligation or punishment," for there is such a thing as sin, but sin is always understood in reference to the spirit of the law of love and liberty. "Everyone who commits sin is a slave. Now the slave's place in the house is not assured, but the son's place is assured. So if the Son makes you free, you will be free indeed" (Jn 8:34–36).

Certainly the freedom of the children of God is essentially and directly an interior freedom, but we have just seen that it should also be inscribed in deeds. Nothing, therefore, that tends to abolish man's alienation is a matter of indifference in the conquest of the total freedom of humanity.

Is it not, moreover, a fire of love, drawn by a great current of profound and truly human freedom, that kindles and flashes like lightning through the code of the new law, synthesizing the whole evangelical politics: the Sermon on the Mount with its catalog of Beatitudes and solemn warnings (Lk 6:20–26; Mt 5:3–48, 6, 7:26; Lk 6:37–49, 13:24)?

4

INDIFFERENTISM AND INCARNATION

If we can affirm, at the end of this analysis, that the Kingdom of God, even while being transcendent, also shows the necessities of political incarnation, would we not be able to conclude that the "world" and its politics are abandoned to their spirit and their laws, especially as, in the first part of our inquiry, we detected a certain indifference to the powers of this world?

In fact, however, that is far from the case: the Gospel is neither theocratic or confusionist nor nevertheless disincarnate or detached, and the fact that the politics of the Church or of Christians has often oscillated between these two errors means simply that the points of application of the two divergent tendencies exist. We have seen our Lord and his doctrine sometimes remain somewhat removed in regard to politics and sometimes become profoundly involved in it—but not at all indifferently. The two kingdoms are distinct, and yet the Kingdom of Heaven implies a certain political "economy." Let us try briefly to recapitulate our analysis and get a clear picture of the dialectial doctrine of the Gospel.

On the one hand, Jesus rejected theocracy and cae-saropapism,[1] the confusion of the political and the religious. When we become more aware of what is being rejected, however, we recognize that it is in the field of what should be called formal politics, which almost corresponds to "superstructure" in the Marxist vocabulary—that is, to the economy as *system of representation*. At this level we are dealing with types of power, organizational system, admin-istration, government, law. Here the Gospel still tends to keep its distance, for this is the emanation of the world as it is, with both good and bad elements. To this world of formal politics, the Gospel complies only with a certain lofty indifference. Let us recall key instances already dis-cussed: this was the case with Pilate, Caiaphas, the Sanhed-rin, the law, and taxation as the sign of allegiance to the power of government.

However, when we enter into concrete and substantial reality (on the level of what Marx called structure, the economy as reality), we see that the evangelical teaching is completely incarnated, entirely political (at the same time and in the same action being entirely religious), with a very precise doctrine. It teaches the primacy of love, the pri-macy of the poor, the communion of goods; no more war, no more enemies, no more violence, the end of the domina-tion of money, perhaps even the end of judgments; help for the weak, the sick, and the afflicted; the obligation of a very pure and demanding individual and social moral con-duct; the primacy of the spiritual, and so on. It is no longer a question, at this level, of a dualism of morality and poli-tics. Christ has come to bring *the* new law, which we must

[1] Theocracy and caesaropapism resemble each other in that they both establish a world in which politics and religion finally become one and the same. The difference between them is that in the latter the secular leader usurps religious power, whereas in the former the pontiff assumes temporal power.

follow completely, with our whole being; the whole man
must be engaged in it (including his social nature) if we
want the world to be saved.[2]

But it will be said that in this way the Gospel is surreptitiously reintroducing a new theocratic spirit. This is not at
all true, however, for the genetic or historical factor should
also be at work. When it takes up the problems of genuine
politics, the Gospel is monist, because, finally, only the
Kingdom of God is of real concern to it, because this is the
Truth and the future of the world. This is a future that has
already begun but remains future. In order that the Kingdom arrive in a definitive manner, a long evolution and ma-
turing process are necessary. Only when the grain is
completely ripe can there be the harvest, the ingathering,
the Parousia. At this point we continue to live with a dual-
istic structure; one part of the world is undergoing a
gradual fermentation, and the other part is the yeast that
causes the fermentation, the tiny flock preparing the future

---

[2] Here we must take a position against the misinterpretation
that is sometimes made of Luke 12:13–14. In this situation Jesus
had been called upon, by one of his listeners, to intervene in a dispute
regarding a family inheritance: " 'Master, tell my brother to give
me a share of our inheritance.' 'My friend,' he replied, 'who appointed me your judge, or the arbitrator of your claims?' "

This text has sometimes been used to prove that the Church
should not intervene in economics and politics. But this is inaccurate. The examination of the true meaning of the pericope and
its context shows that Christ's answer has two distinct levels:

1. It is not for me to make the division—a position supporting
the distinction between the spiritual and the temporal (against
theocracy).

2. The division ought to be made in conformity with the principles of my law, emphasizing justice and especially detachment
from property. In fact, the succeeding verses are given over to the
parable of the foolish rich man; there is, therefore, a truly Christian position and solution of the problem presented. The distinction of levels is not equivalent to a disincarnation.

kingdom. Until the Parousia, we ought to think, live, and act as Jesus—that is, without any theocratic intention. The Church will be theocratic only after the Parousia, for at that time the two kingdoms, that of God and that of the world, will coincide, and there will be but one. The world will have become a new world. There will be but one flock and one shepherd.

But again, we must be on our guard. What we have just said does not mean that when one is a disciple of Christ, he does not have to try to apply the political law of God's kingdom. On the contrary, if you do not follow the law of Christ concretely, here and now, in the world, how can you look forward to the day when there will be only one flock and one shepherd? Who will follow this law, and when? The end of humanity is the coming together, the coincidence of the two kingdoms. But the new Kingdom is already in the making, and it is up to us to work in the direction of this coincidence. Certainly, we cannot claim that the final coming together will be simply the fruit of a maturation process; too many texts of Christ speak of wars, cataclysms, and the weakening of faith at the crucial hour. But the Gospel is a ferment and a seed in the midst of this world. In the "Our Father" we ask God, at Christ's invitation, "Thy Kingdom come, thy will be done, on earth as it is in Heaven" (Mt 6:10). This coming has begun with Revelation; it ought to continue. In the fullest sense we may say that the law of universal love (with all that flows from this in detail) *is* the law of the world that from now on is in the process of becoming, because this is what it *ought* to be and what it *will* be.

A keen understanding of the present point, we may note in passing, explains (without excusing) the old theocratic error. If we wished to put the best interpretation on the matter, we would say that through an excess of apostolic zeal men imagine themselves to be constructing, immediately and completely, the City of God here on earth.[3] Such zeal is sadly unenlightened, because the Kingdom of God here below is established only in a very preliminary fashion, and if we are following the Gospel, there can be no question of advancing it by utilizing the weapons of darkness: force, deception, war, confusion. We can advance the Kingdom only by giving witness, by concretely transforming the political structures of society in the direction of the Gospel, but without trying to destroy the "world" before God gives the order for it.

We can say that the Revelation, from the political point of view with which we are concerned, starts out (with the Old Testament) from a coincidence of confusion in the duality between the two kingdoms and comes to completion in the Parousia, a coincidence of fusion in unity. Between one and the other of these terms, the politics of the Gospel presupposes the respect, in detachment, for the world, whose autonomy it recognizes, while at the same time demanding of its disciples an active perfection capable of hastening the arrival of the Kingdom until the final unity.

Supported by what we discovered in the previous paragraphs, the disciple of Christ can and ought to consider that *all* evangelical teaching, even that which specifically in the text has a spiritual application, necessarily also postulates a concrete political application (by virtue of the fact that the law of the Kingdom is incarnated and that it is potentially the law of the world to come); thus he can and ought to

---

[3] This confusion will be especially understandable at the beginning of the fourth century, when, in the euphoria of religious peace and a prince who favored Christianity and in an atmosphere still bathed in eschatological excitement, Christians believed that the Roman empire was the image and even the realization of God's Kingdom already arrived.

draw consequences from this and practical political decisions, always respecting, of course, evangelical imperatives when determining the manner of proceeding. It is thus that the Church has applied Christ's spirit of assistance to the sick and the needy and, by transposition, to the teaching of children. It is in the same terms that internationalization is seen as a political corollary of the order "Preach to every creature" without distinction of race; that juridical and political equality is a transposition of that religious equality preached by the Gospel; the same point may be made in regard to freedom, love, solidarity, fraternity, and so on. In all this, and by means of all this, God is at work, and His Kingdom comes closer to realization. This is the implicit politics of the Gospel.

In the face of these two series of evangelical texts that we have passed in review—one that directly contains instruction in the area of politics and another that is specifically religious but is also able to, and ultimately ought to, find its political application—we cannot prevent ourselves from asking what becomes of the necessary autonomy of the economic, social, and political sciences and techniques.

The answer, it seems, has four parts. First, the evangelical distinction between the two kingdoms, on the level of formal politics, allows for complete liberty as regard to systems, or what might be called superstructures.[4] Second, it is,

---

[4] Besides, if it is necessary to distinguish between political reality itself, as constituted by effective economic and social relationships (how, in fact, men are fed, get along with each other, and form themselves into groups; how they act with each other on every level) and the various formalities under which this reality may be represented (patriarchate, tyranny, oligarchy, republic, monarchy, democracy, as well as the different structures of these various systems, such as assemblies, elections, delegations, cabinets), it is none the less true that a permanent dialectic goes on beneath the relationships between this reality and its representations. The latter can not be considered empty forms, with the former constituting a kind of substantial magma, living but inexpressible; nor

however, symptomatic and curious that the Gospel, so concrete and incarnate, basically attaches very little real importance to the political world as a system of representation;
this merits some reflection. Third, there is nothing to
prevent the Christian, Gospel in his head as well as in his
heart, from necessarily guiding these techniques in a particular direction. And, finally, there is nothing to prevent this
direction from being that of God's Kingdom.

We see, then, that there is no contradiction. Evangelical
indifferentism certainly exists, and the Catholic Church in a
certain way has always preserved this tradition, sometimes
to the point of scandalizing Catholics themselves. Empires,
monarchies, republics—basically the Church attaches little
importance to these various forms of power, recognizing all
of them without being committed to them. If a major development takes place, it will gather information from both
sides and come to an agreement with whichever side comes
out on top. But it is not for that we can reproach the
Church—at least, not in the name of the Gospel. Its role
and its domain are situated on another level.

Nevertheless, it should also be noted that the interior
movement of Christian renewal as described by the Gospel
—love, justice, fraternity, liberty, pardon, an attitude to
money and the poor, and so on—involves the whole man
and all his activities and ought to produce its fruits *ad extra*
in all areas. It is on this level that evangelical action is situ-

are the latter pure representations, with the former a pure noume-
nal reality. The latter efficaciously signify (in part) a reality about
which, without them, nothing much could be known or said or
done. Indispensable, they are nevertheless always imperfect and inadequate because the reality they express, structure, and organize
is too rich with concrete life (involving the whole rational animal
inasmuch as he cannot live by himself) to be able to be fully
validated in a series of rational propositions.

It is obvious that evangelical indifferentism applies only to
formal politics insofar as it is inadequate and constantly out of
date, not in its involvement with human social foundations.

ated, or ought to be. In this sense, we should return to John 18:36 and understand well that Jesus' answer to Pilate implies that his Kingdom does not originate in this world, not that it should not be built up and propagated *in* this world. It is a mystical, moral, and spiritual Kingdom, although completely incarnate.

It is at this level, also, that all too often we are forced to deplore the failure of Christians. If all Christians—not all those who are sociologically Christian, but simply all convinced Christians—became impregnated with evangelical morality and practiced it, it is absolutely certain that Holy Mother Church, the *Catholikê* of Christians, would constitute a remarkable spiritual power that would shake the world to its diseased roots and drain most of its social and international abcesses. The obviousness of this fact carries in itself a terrible condemnation for all of us who stand up every Sunday in church to listen to "the continuation of the holy Gospel," the holy word, for as long as the Gospel does not haunt our political existence.

II
THE AVATARS OF
EVANGELICAL
POLITICS

5

THE PRIMITIVE CHURCH
AND THE FATHERS

At the end of our analysis of the political thought of the Gospel, it is quite natural to wonder what has become of this tradition, both in the Church and in the world. Besides, with the aim of examining some tendencies and essential points of resistance of Christian politics today to arrive at a few propositions for immediate action, it would seem useful to establish the liaison between two aspects—the historic Gospel and actuality—in order to understand better how the latter could result from the former. Intellectual curiosity and explanatory usefulness come together, therefore, to demand a historical survey of the centuries that, after the preaching of the Gospel, preceded the political action of the Christians of our time.

Unfortunately, the length of this essay makes it necessary for this survey to be all too brief.[1] A proper study of

---

[1] It is even more rapid than another survey, undertaken from another point of view, in my essay on the Gospel (*Quelle est donc cette Bonne Nouvelle?* [1961], pp. 81–152), in which I was more concerned with the intellectual aspect of the destiny of the Gospel over the course of centuries.

our subject would require us to be able to follow closely and in detail the avatars of the political doctrine of the Gospel during the course of ages—on one hand, in the thought of the Fathers and the theologians and, on the other hand, in action, in the life of the Church, in its effective behavior in the face of political problems. This work would be of the highest utility but would require numerous volumes and a whole team of scholars. Here we do possess neither that possibility nor that ambition; thus we shall be content to sketch out a unifying line between what we have just discovered in the Gospel and the problems with which we are presented today, in the second half of the twentieth century, so that the confrontation between them will be more comprehensive. We shall then limit ourselves to presenting a few rare landmarks from the long course of history, moving along by means of quick sketches and hasty suggestions, chosen sometimes from the world of ideas, sometimes from active life, in order to characterize very summarily a few of the types of society that have succeeded each other in two thousand years and a few of the various patterns of behavior that Christians have invented, both for good and for evil, for their guidance in the interior of these societies.

Saint Paul

The first great theologian of the Church, Saint Paul, deserves almost as important an analysis as the evangelical text itself. His fidelity to the doctrine of Jesus is total.

At the level of formal politics, the great text of the epistle to the Romans (13:1–7) repeats the thesis of submission to the civil power and its divine origin:

You must all obey the governing authorities. Since all government comes from God, the civil authorities were appointed by God, and so anyone who resists authority is rebelling against

God's decision, and such an act is bound to be punished. . . .
This is also the reason why you must pay taxes, since all government officials are God's officers. They serve God by col-
lecting taxes. Pay every government official what he has a
right to ask—whether it be direct tax or indirect, fear or
honor.[2]

But the poet of charity has rightly seen that the latter has
transformed the reality of concrete politics from top to
bottom. For example, "there are no more distinctions between . . . slave and free" (Gal 3:28); all are equally sons
of God, co-heirs of Jesus Christ, and "are one in Christ
Jesus." Thus, all men are equally called to the Kingdom;
there is no longer "neither Greek nor Jew" (Col 4:9–12; 1
Co 12:13), and it is only because of concern for apostolic
effectiveness and in a spirit of deferential indifference that
the Apostle of the Gentiles would one day plead an exception, before the authorities, in the name of his Roman citizenship. The Roman citizen and former doctor of the law
Saul has become Paul, a Pharisee who will not hesitate to
work with his hands, like the humblest of artisans, to make
camel-hair tents (Acts 18:3).

All this is in the direct line of evangelical teaching, as is
the Pauline position in regard to civil justice. The latter is
especially given expression in Corinthians (1 Co 6:1–12),
where three chief points are stressed: the moral and religious condemnation of wrongdoing ("The unjust will certainly not inherit the Kingdom of God"); condemnation
of passing judgment on wrongdoers ("It is bad enough for

[2] Peter says the same thing in his first epistle: "For the sake
of the Lord, accept the authority of every social institution: the
emperor, as the supreme authority, and the governors as commis-
sioned by him to punish criminals and praise good citizenship.
. . . You are slaves of no one except God, so behave like free men,
and never use your freedom as an excuse for wickedness. Have
respect for everyone and love for our community; fear God and
honor the emperor" (2:13–17).

you to have lawsuits at all against one another: oughtn't you to let yourselves be wronged, and let yourselves be cheated?"); finally, if one wishes at all costs to pass judgment, at least let it not be before civil courts with judges who "were not even respected in the Church" but between Christians, before "one reliable man among you to settle differences between brothers." This last point is only a concession; the absolute of evangelical law remains that among brothers one does not judge.

This absolute, which is that of universal love, extends, as in the words of Christ, even to the denial of the idea of enemy (Rom 12:14–21), just as it tended, as we have seen, to efface every difference of class, race, and nation.

Economic and Social Incarnation

This same active law informs the life of the young Church from its origin and gives rise to the most original economic, social, and political realizations, which were at the same time most characteristic of evangelical doctrine when rigorously followed. Thus, from the beginning the faithful placed all things in common: "The whole group of believers was united, heart and soul; no one claimed for his use anything that he had, as everything they owned was held in common. . . . None of their members was ever in want, as all those who owned land or houses would sell them, and bring the money from them, to present it to the apostles; it was then distributed to any members who might be in need" (Acts 4:32–35). Moreover, in the aftermath, in the face of the difficulties of organization and distribution that arose, the community chose seven of its brothers as specialists in the service of administration and relief. These are the deacons (Acts 6:1–6); they would have associates (deaconesses)—although, it is true, for only a short time—often widows, more especially dedicated to the care of the sick, the assistance of the needy, and the education of children. We grasp here, almost in the pure state, the phenomenon of creation of a socioeconomic structure through strict application of the Gospel's instructions and fruitful invention in the direction of absolute love. What the first Christians thus discovered was a socialism before its time: the community of goods and equality, specialization and planning, with attribution according to needs, assistance to children and the down-and-out, and the destruction of the reign of money.

We discover, in the recruitment of the first Christians, this same vigorous incarnation of evangelical precepts. Especially at the outset, it was truly the lowest of the lowest on the social ladder who were converted. Saint Paul told the Corinthians: "Brothers, at the time when you were called: how many of you were wise in the ordinary sense of the word, how many were influential people, or came from noble families?" (1 Co 1:26) Much later, Celsus thought he would disparage Christians by waxing ironical about their recruitment of "carders, shoemakers, and fullers," and Minucius Felix (Octavius 8, 3) summed up the objections of pagans with these words: "They grub among the dregs of the populace for ignorant folk and make conspirators of them." Even in the middle of the third century Origen was not afraid to admit that the Church was recruited essentially from "among weavers, fullers, and shoemakers."

But there were still slaves. We have seen what Pauline doctrine was; without alteration or concession, it has been practiced by the Church. The Apostle himself gave instruction to Philemon, from whose home the slave Onesimus had fled; with all the gentleness of which this passionate heart was capable, he wanted to lead Philemon voluntarily to accept that Onesimus should no longer be received as a slave, but as "a very dear brother." It is necessary to reread that whole paragraph of the epistle to Philemon (8–21), which in fact was the reason for the letter and in which Paul used the warm and fraternal power of persuasion, although he delicately pointed out at the beginning that he could not impose his views as an obligation.

This way of doing things was typical of the style of the Church at that time: The Church did not formally condemn slavery or attack the institution directly but, by rejecting what constituted its ideological foundation, emptied it of its substance. In this way Christians, despite their feeble strength in the empire and their practice of submission to power, performed revolutionary acts: by recognizing the marriage of slaves, by rejecting the rights of the master, and by helping to bring about an increasing number of emancipations.

Political Commitment

The incarnation of love extended to the whole of politics. In fact, the first Christians did not limit themselves to applying the principles of evangelical politics to the internal organization of the Church, where obviously they dominated their whole life—the leaders of the Church were truly the "servants" of the others, and the bishop himself would for some time remain strictly linked to his presbytery. The expression "See how they love one another" was not then a stylistic clause or a pious souvenir of folklore but a grudging tribute that pagans uttered in sheer amazement.

This effective love was extended to things *ad extra*. For example, applying in the most literal terms the evangelical precept of not knowing even the idea of enemy, one could see Christians who had just escaped the persecution of Decius immediately go out and voluntarily sacrifice themselves in offering assistance to a plague-ridden city or to an area ravaged by earthquake.

But what especially impressed the pagans was that this religion (which welcomed everyone without distinction of race, blood, or class and which was so strangely transforming the behavior of its faithful) refused to become part of the syncretism that combined official worship and Oriental religions. For those who did not possess the key of the Gospel, the Christians certainly seemed strange people. At the same time, they were seen participating in the life of the city; some of them even served the emperor in his legions; others were quite soon found in administrative and government posts, sometimes at the imperial court.

But they were citizens both fully committed and half in secession. Undoubtedly, as the author of the epistle to Diognetus remarked at the end of the second century, Christ's faithful did not differ from other men of their class in their clothes, their food, or their houses; and Tertullian, at least at the outset, was able to write: "We do not live withdrawn from this world, like you, we frequent the forum, the baths, the workshops, the stores, the markets, the public squares; we practice the professions of sailor, soldier, farmer, shop-keeper; we place our work and industry at your service." Yes, all this was true, but there were, nevertheless, certain areas where they were not to be found, for example, the circus and the temples; because these establishments were part of the social and political structure of the country, this absence was resented as a reproach and a rejection. In effect, it was one: the rejection of the world, of cruelty, of the worship of the Caesars, of pagan theocracy! Similarly, they rejected luxury and impurity, and they were almost alone in rejecting on principle carnal relations outside of marriage.

Some even considered an active revolutionary program against the new Babylon, or at least became conscientious objectors by opposing conscription. Of course, this was the position of a very small number (and, moreover, military service was not obligatory under the empire); it is also true that the hierarchy, whether because of patriotism in the case of military service or its concern to preserve the Gospel teaching of nonviolence in its purity (that is, free from any relationship to proposals for revolt) did not support these extremists. Nevertheless, it remains true that all this indicates the fidelity of Christians to a religious ideal that was solidly incarnated and proudly affirmed, especially in that they did not hesitate, in order to safeguard it, to go to their death.

Ultimately, therefore, Christians remained rather disturbing citizens. Despite their respect and obedience, pagans were able to reproach them for the limits of this obedience and the moderation of their passion for the salvation and expansion of the empire.

Limits of Evangelical Politics

Nevertheless, from the point of view of the Gospel, were not Christians still too submissive to the State in certain areas? It would be presumptuous to criticize witnesses who got themselves murdered and who, in addition, admirably understood and practiced the political doctrine of the Gospel immeasurably better than any of their successors. But our purpose here is not to criticize; what is indispensable is to try to see exactly what parts of the Gospel did not immediately pass over into the life of the Church, as well as those things that, alas, were rapidly abandoned after having been once applied.

The most noteworthy of their frontier points undoubtedly concerns military service. The hierarchy of the primitive Church was perhaps right, for reasons that we have suggested, to be suspicious of those enthusiasts who practiced or wished to practice conscientious objection. It is none the less true that the direction taken at that moment, which for centuries would commit the Church to another path, did not conform to either the letter or the spirit of the Gospel. In our view, therefore, there is reason to regret that the refusal to kill (apart from the circus, or on the battlefield) was not added, in this age of grace, heroic courage, and fidelity, to the numerous other rejections through which our first brethren opposed the spirit of the world. Unhappily, they did not perceive things in that light or they would not have hesitated; they looked without suspicion at what seemed only an element of the everyday social world—at a time, moreover, when humanity was so little planetarized that they had no inkling of the relativity of the idea of fatherland in comparison with other values.

Even more, with the passage of time, many of the rigors would be lessened, to the great misfortune of strict evangelical doctrine. In the domain of economics, the total community of goods would be forgotten by the end of the third century (and, undoubtedly, well before then), leaving behind (which is already a great deal, it is true) only a certain suspicion of money, of excessive display in women's toilet, and of riches in general. There also survived (which is more important) very severe prescriptions concerning the acquisition and use of material goods. From the very first centuries (in fact, at the Council of Elvira moneylending would have a bad reputation, which it was to retain for a long time in Christian countries, being considered directly contrary to the spirit of love and reciprocal giving proper to the Gospel.

We are forced to recognize that this relative relaxation of evangelical purity coincided with the extension, in quantity, of Christianity and with the conversion of elements close to the administration of the empire and even in the imperial council. Even under Nero we have seen some conquests among the aristocracy (such as Pomponia Graecina), and under Vespasian and Titus there was a movement to win over the ruling classes and even the entourage of the emperors, so that it can be pointed out that two hundred years before Constantine the empire was almost headed by Flavius Clemens, first cousin of Titus and Domitian, and his wife, Flavia Domitilla, a Christian prince and princess. Besides, starting with Hadrian and especially in the second half of the second century, Christianity began to penetrate the educated circles. Certainly, among the members of the Roman senatorial aristocracy, the high bourgeoisie of the provinces, the liberal professions (magistrates, lawyers), matrons from good families, there were both men and women saints—and even well-known martyrs: Gregory of Neo-Caesarius, Cyprian of Carthage, and many others.

It would be fatuous to regret that conversions took place among the aristocracy, but the consequence of this development was that Christianity ran the risk of surrendering to the temptation of making itself comfortable, becoming more temporally established, and forgetting in its day-to-day existence that salvation belongs to the poor and the humble. Did it always keep in mind that the doctrine and the Church of love, if it ought to remain free and independent on the level of formal politics even while conceding a sincere but limited obedience to the State, ought also, on the contrary, to incarnate itself, to materialize vigorously towards and against everything, at the level of real politics? The answer has a name, which is (and it may be regretted from more than one viewpoint) that of Constantine.

The Fathers of the Church

Earlier, it would have been interesting to consider, on both sides of the great Constantinian failure, how the interpretation of evangelical political thought took place on the intellectual level. Unfortunately, we are unable to pursue this avenue of reflection, partly because the inquiry is, if not deceptive, at least clearly less rewarding than that bearing on the life of the Church and especially because it would take up enormous space. During the very earliest period, the fathers, when they did not refer to the State with the ignominious and apocalyptic term "the Beast," made an attempt (especially the apologetic fathers of the second century, but also others in the third) to reduce the gap dividing the world and the Gospel and to show that Christians are good citizens.

But are not both these positions too simplistic? We do not always rediscover in them what impressed us in the attitude of Christ, at once firm and nuanced, in his encounters with "Caesar."

Turned toward the apocalyptic perspectives of the Kingdom "to come" or concerned to underline the radical renewal that the inauguration of the Kingdom had already accomplished in the Incarnation event, the foundation of the Church, the fathers generally found themselves caught up, so to speak, in a climate completely alien to that of God's "coming" Kingdom.

Meditating on the Gospel in connection with interior demands of the spiritual life, they were little attuned to the political implications that flow from it; in addition, they were often more preoccupied by problems of speculative theology and the struggle against heresies.

The tendencies that characterized the great theological schools of the Greek Church also influenced the way they interpreted those words and actions of Jesus discussed in our first two chapters, especially on the subject of wealth; with his predilection for spiritual exegesis, Clement of Alexandria would give an interpretation of them from which people could take an orientation favorable to a humanism stressing the "happy medium." He affirmed, nevertheless, the transcendence of the Christian mystery over Greek wisdom, but he also entered into such distinctions as to provide a kind of authorization to attenuate the folly of the Cross and the appeal to stretch one's personal limits and to overthrow generally accepted values—in brief, the claim of the absolute in the love of God and of others. On the contrary, Saint John Chrysostom, although he lived in a Church that was far more established, spoke with a great deal more vigor, bringing out into the open the violently "oppositionist" character of evangelical behavior. One could rediscover the same differences between these two great doctors of the Church on the subject of the love of enemies.[3]

[3] For my details, see again *Quelle est donc cette Bonne Nouvelle?* pp. 95–103.

6

FROM CONSTANTINE TO CHARLEMAGNE

Whether it was an accommodation or a sign of fatigue, the mirage of power or a matter of growing old, or, in the case of the fathers, the bankruptcy of theologians, the fact remains that the peace of Constantine revealed itself, regarding the application of the political doctrine of the Gospel, as heavy with unhappy and lasting consequences of the political doctrine of the Gospel, as heavy with unhappy and lasting consequences from which we have not yet stopped suffering.

Nevertheless, if we may indulge in the somewhat empty game of "it might have been," we cannot keep ourselves from dreaming . . . It all might have taken place this way: we would be able to conceive of the possibility that the edict of Milan, a simple *exeat* ("We wish," it said, "that whoever desires to follow the Christian religion should be able to do so without any fear of being troubled"), might have marked the beginning of a long regime under which the State, while maintaining its own autonomy, would have allowed the Church to act, and the latter would have profited from the facilities granted it by transforming structures and leading humanity to advance with great strides toward the total Christ. In itself, the edict of Milan could have inaugurated a system perfectly in accord with the indifferentism of the Gospel in the domain of formal politics, as well as with the action of Christians at the level of day-to-day politics.

But we know what happened. In a climate of euphoria, men believed that the Kingdom had arrived; now there was but one Heaven and one earth; the emperor was the prince of goodness, the good worker for the coming harvest— why would he not come to the aid of the Church? The Church allowed itself to be unburdened of a part of its prerogatives; the caesaropapism of emperors Constantine I, Constantine II, Justinian, Justin II, Constant II, and Leo III encroached on the most spiritual powers of the pope and the bishops in making decisions in dogmatic questions. The result was confusion even among the best: Ambrose of Milan called for the freedom of the Church in vigorous terms ("Divine things are not subject to imperial power") and proclaimed that the emperor's place was in the interior of the Church, not above it (and Ambrose treated Theodosius as a public sinner because of the latter's massacre of thousands of rioters), but he also affirmed that the civil power should not tolerate the exercise of a heretical cult of Jewish expansion. There was the same split in Augustine, who, in attacking African Donatism, asked for the support of "the secular arm."

The Gospel, transformed into the official religion, became linked with a decadent empire, and the evangelization of the non-Roman world was carried on in Asia in great confusion. In the West, the whole process came to a head with Charlemagne, of whom it might be said that "he established the bridge that linked up ancient caesaropapism and modern Gallicanism." In reality he too would not hesitate to settle doctrinal controversies and make decisions regard-

ing the reform of the liturgy, just as Byzantine emperors
were accustomed to doing.[1] Besides, after the chaotic time
of the Merovingians, the Carolingian age was to see the
consolidation of clerical privileges (fiscal and juridical ex-
emptions and the birth and development of Church property).

In this way the status that Constantine and Theodosius
had given the Church of Jesus Christ became fixed and
rigid. This poisoned gift not only affected the level of "formal" politics (the Church, no longer practicing evangelical
indifferentism in regard to political structures, sanctified a
particular regime) but also brought on more and more serious surrenders of principle at the level of "real" politics:
attitudes in regard to money, violence, liberty, and universalism.

Nevertheless, on this same level, all was not forgotten:
the Church made its public debut in a role that was to last
for a long time: The teacher and civilizer of humanity.[2]
All during the fourth century, the Constantinian legislation
from 315 to 324, then the laws of Gratian and Theodosius,
gave formal recognition to the influence of evangelical
morality on the official and juridical life of the world,
softening the fate of condemned criminals, and protecting
the feeble, minors, the innocent, slaves and orphans. In addition, the Church began to give a gentler tone to public
manners; in times of both peace and war, as well as to in-

---

[1] One example, among others, of this confusion: in 775 a priest
named Cathaulf wrote Charlemagne: "Remember God, in fear and
love, since He is your king and you are His representative to protect and govern the members of His Church. . . . The bishop
comes second; he is only the representative of Christ" (*Mon.
Germn. Historiae Epistolae*, IV, p. 503).

[2] This is what might be called the substitute function of the
Church. In various areas, such as education, care for the needy, and
improvement of manners, it takes over the role of a state that was
rather delinquent than incompetent.

struct children and take on a responsibility for culture and to render assistance to the sick and the destitute. All of this, alas, was not enough to compensate for fundamental failures in political responsibility.

7

THE MIDDLE AGES

From Caesaropapism to Theocracy

Whereas in the East the Christian empire established by Constantine, Theodosius, and Justinian was to survive, for better or worse, for a thousand years, the West, which had thought it was seeing "a new Constantine" appearing in 800, floundered, both before and after Charlemagne, into a collapse of political power. General anarchy meant a return to near-barbarism, and one result was a general state of immorality that even affected the clergy, at all levels of the hierarchy.

In the face of this decadence in both State and Church, some popes, bishops, priests, and monks—even some of the most disinterested, purest, and best intentioned—were led either to assume for themselves certain direct responsibilities in the political order (to fill a vacuum) or to give approval to the secular powers when the latter attempted to bring back a little order to society and the Church, which at that time could scarcely be distinguished. Indeed, there were genuine saints, filled with evangelical virtues, who rejoiced to see an Otto the Great or a Saint Henry take over the direction, as emperors, of the reform of the clergy and of ecclesiastical institutions that had been poisoned by many abuses.

More frequently, however, caesaropapism, which had become traditional and had been made worse by the feudal relationships of vassal to suzerain, encouraged these abuses by making Church authorities dependent on lay princes; the latter came to choose bishops and abbots themselves, Gods knows according to what criteria! As a result, the reformist popes of the eleventh century were led to wage a fierce fight to get back these "investitures" from civil power. The restoration of evangelical virtues among the clergy was greatly conditioned by this recovery, without which it had proved impossible.

We know what a dramatic turn this quarrel took with the memorable encounter at Canossa. It was in this climate that Gregory VII drew up the *Dictatus papae* in 1075, which placed the pope at the summit of human society and attributed to him the imperial insignia and the power of deposing emperors.

These pretensions to theocracy (or, more precisely, to priestly government) were opposed, somewhat inconsistently, to those of caesaropapism, to which the restoration of Roman law very opportunely gave an ideological foundation. But while the legalists were in this way bringing us closer to the totalitarian state, in imitation of pagan Rome, the clergy, except for some conciliators like Yves of Chartres, were elaborating from their side a canonical construction that was just as "molar." Basing their position especially on a (fake) donation of Constantine (again!), they wanted to make the emperor the instrument, the secular arm, of the pope.

"The Sovereign Pontiff is the head of the Church. The king is only his right hand," proclaimed Innocent III at the beginning of the thirteenth century. Innocent II had already had a fresco painted that showed Lothair of Supplimbourg on his knees before the pope, and the legend made its point very clearly: "The king comes in front of the gates; he swears first of all to respect the privileges of Rome, then he becomes the pope's man and receives the crown that the pope gives him."

We thus come to the celebrated claim of "the two swords" by Boniface VII in his bull *Unam sanctam*. Honoré of Autun had already formulated its principle in the twelfth century: "For the government of the Church, in this present life, the Lord has shown that two swords were necessary: the spiritual sword that the priesthood uses against sinners and the material sword that royalty uses to punish stubborn criminals." [1]

Fifty years before Boniface VII, Innocent IV, in the middle of his struggle with Frederick II, had been just as radical in his bull *Eger cui levia* (1245):

Whoever attempts to withdraw from the authority of the Vicar of Christ . . . by this very act commits an offense against the authority of Christ himself. The King of Kings has established us on earth as his universal representative and has conferred on us the fullness of power by giving, first to the

---

[1] It should be pointed out that this theory of the two swords rests on an unfounded interpretation of Luke 22:35–38, in which Jesus, on the night before his arrest, spoke of the universal hostility his disciples will meet, advising them, "But now if you have a purse, take it; if you have a haversack, do the same; if you have no sword, sell your cloak and buy one." The disciples did not understand him and replied, "Lord, there are two swords here now." Then Jesus decided there was no point in insisting and abruptly broke off the conversation: "That is enough."

It is hard to understand how this passage could have led to such confusion, especially in view of Jesus' explicit commandment of nonviolence, which was presented in our analysis of evangelical politics and is well summarized in Matthew 26:53: "All who draw the sword will die by the sword."

prince of the apostles and then to us, the power to bind and to loose not only whoever but whatever it may be. . . . The Roman pontiff can exercise his pontifical power over every Christian at least occasionally. . . . The power of temporal government cannot be exercised apart from the Church because there is no power established by God apart from her. . . . Those who imagine that the Apostolic See received the sovereignty of the empire from Constantine lack perception and do not know how to get to the origin of things; the reality, as we know, is that the Church already possessed this sovereignty, by nature and in the state of potency. Our Lord Jesus Christ, son of God, true man and true God, true king and true priest, according to the order of Melchizedek, established for the benefit of the Holy See a monarchy that is not only pontifical but royal; he has handed over to blessed Peter and his successors the reins of empire, both earthly and celestial, as the plurality of the keys indicates. By means of one, as vicar of Christ, the pope has received the power of exercising his jurisdiction over the world in regard to temporal things and by means of the other, over Heaven in regard to spiritual things.

Of course, it can be argued that Boniface VII was simply stating, in however unsympathetic a manner, a permanent truth: that is, that every political act falls under the light of faith and the grasp of grace, but its arguments, drawn out of a deficient theological development, give to this text, as to the bull of Innocent IV, the appearance of a manifesto that is quite foreign to the political doctrine and behavior of the Lord Jesus.

The Crusades and the Inquisition

It is not only the overemphasis on the juridical (by both the curial canonist and the imperial legalist) that weighed on the Middle Ages. From the Carolingian age on, political inspiration seems to have been sought out more in the Old Testament (with overly facile analogies made to the holy wars of Israel!) than in the New.

Add to this the ignorance, however excusable, of geography and ethnology (people believed that the entire universe had already been evangelized), as well as of depth psychology (people could not believe that a heretic was in good faith),[2] keep in mind the pervasive influence of a philosophy more attentive to essences than to the person, and you have the explanation of those things that seem to us today most shocking in the Middle Ages, which in other respects can often be seen as admirable: the Crusades and the Inquisition. . . . Some ten centuries after Christ, there were his disciples, torturing and killing and causing others to torture and kill—for what? To advance the Kingdom of God!

Did those Christians, both clergymen and laymen, who were responsible for those Crusades undertaken to rescue the Holy Sepulcher, did they forget the warning of the angels to the holy women: "Why look among the dead for someone who is alive? He is not here, he is risen" (Lk 24:5). In their eyes, apparently, Christ was truly dead. It is true that to arrive at such an understanding of things, they had to forget the political texts of the Gospel; men had gone far from the Sermon on the Mount; indeed, they had reached its opposite. What was being followed was the diabolical logic of the spirit of this world: the pope is the supreme temporal head of mankind, so why should he not make war for ends that were both temporal and spiritual?

Charlemagne had considered his conquests as religious undertakings, but he was a temporal sovereign. Now the voice of the vicar of Christ was calling for military opera-

---

[2] None of the heretics handed over to the Inquisition had been brought up in heresy since childhood. They had all first belonged to the Church and had abandoned it simply through their own will, by means of a personal decision. At the time people could not imagine how such a decision could be made with a sincere heart without realizing that one was defying God's authority.

tions and promising special graces to those who fought in them, just as Muhammad had done. War appeared to Christians a legitimate way to advance the Kingdom of God. The warrior in Spain as well as the one in Palestine benefited from the remission of his sins, and the expedition called the Second Crusade (1145-1146) took on the appearance of a general offensive of Christendom against the Moslems of Syria and Spain and against the pagan Slavs. The hour was approaching when the Church, if its temporal interests were threatened, would undertake crusades in order to safeguard them.[3]

The crusades once seemed a glorious page in Western Christendom; the chansons de geste and the religious romanticism of the nineteenth century easily idealized this great age of faith. Today we are perhaps better able to notice its terrible ambiguities, even while recognizing that it also gave witness to a sincere effort to subordinate all the activity of a society to a religious purpose maintained by the Church. There is also much reason to regret that, far from reconciling Greeks and Latins, the crusades only aggravated their differences, delaying the unity of Christians and making its achievement more difficult.

Of course, there were men who were able to sanctify themselves in and through the crusades—and even in and through the Inquisition. Nevertheless, how strange all this seems to the evangelical conscience! Now we see the bitter fruit of the grave confusion that marked the entire Middle Ages and has even been prolonged beyond them:

Theologians taught that the pope had the duty to exercise strong supervision over the use that kings made of their temporal power and to require their services when the good of souls was involved. On their side, the legalists, who demanded complete autonomy for the kings in temporal affairs, were no less positive in claiming that the royal power was very partic-

[3] Bernard Guillemin, *The Later Middle Ages* (1960), p. 43.

ularly intended for the glorification and defense of the faith. How, then, would the religious and civil authorities not be in agreement in resisting heresy? [4]

Whatever the case, the attempts of Catholic apologists to justify the crusades and the Inquisition are, in one sense, almost more painful than these errors themselves.

For ourselves, we do not wish to bring to trial the past of a Church that would then play the role of the accused, as if the Gospel had been completely absent from its life since the time of Constantine! We are only mentioning objective errors, generally located at the level of structures and outlooks that are created by the play of history rather than by individual sentiments and choices.

To say this, however, is not to excuse everything ahead of time, for these structures and group attitudes constitute

[4] See G. Courtade, S.J., "A propos de la liberté religieuse," *Cahiers d'action religieuse et sociale* (July 1-15, 1965). Reflection on the forthcoming solemn declaration of the council (already delayed several times), the author asks if this position can be reconciled with discipline of the Church toward heretics in antiquity and during the Middle Ages, and his answer seems quite accurate: "The Middle Ages made a sacral conception of civil society. People were living under a regime of Christendom. The profession of Catholic faith was part of the definition of a citizen. Church and State, the religious society and the civil society, interpenetrated; they did not form two distinct societies but one, both spiritual and temporal. Under these conditions, heresy was looked at not simply from the religious point of view as apostasy but simultaneously as a crime against society. It undermined the bases of order; it broke the cohesion of government; today we would say that it destroyed the social contract. This was so true that kings and princes often showed themselves more rigorous in stamping out heresy than popes and bishops. They reproached the sovereign pontiff for not adopting sufficiently energetic measures for this purpose. Those heretics judged as stubborn by the Inquisition were condemned to death by lay tribunals, not simply by virtue of their heresy but because heresy was a grave attack against the common weal, as it was then understood, and threatened the safety of the State as it then existed and as, according to the general consensus, it ought to be" (*ibid.*, p. 419).

part of our responsibilities and also have repercussions on our intentions and feelings. Thus, the theocratic situation, it would seem, carries with it grave risks of deviation, and its exercise has brought into play various feelings and intentions. It remains true, nevertheless, that very often the intention of those responsible was honorable; they sincerely willed the good of men, the reign of Christ, and the triumph of goodness and justice.

However, our faith does not forbid us from assuming that there was also serious sin, in the proper sense of the word, in the behavior of certain churchmen and on every level of the hierarchy. As Rahner has written, "There is no dogma according to which the inspiration of the Holy Spirit, which is always with the Church, would restrict this influence of sin in Church leaders and not permit it to invade the area of their work in the Church." [5]

Another German Jesuit theologian, Jungmann, has given us the same warning quite recently:

The Church "upholds the truth and keeps it safe," of course, for this is an essential part of the power with which it has been endowed. Nevertheless, this does not exclude the possibility that deficiencies will be manifested in the proclamation of this truth. Although holy, the Church remains none the less marked by a large number of human failures. We would, moreover, never be able to say that it had need of reforms, recollection, and renewal if the inadequacies of its members did not manifest themselves from time to time in secondary domains. It is necessary always to maintain that this inadequacy may arise from the mediocrity of its leaders as well as that of its humble followers, from their lack of openness of mind, their faintheartedness, excessive or insufficient adaptation to the demands of the age—in brief, from attitudes that depend on the limits of human talents and perhaps would not imply any culpability. We must always expect such deficiencies, especially

[5] Karl Rahner, "The Church of Sinners," *Cross Currents* (Spring 1951), p. 69.

because more culpable failures even in the direction of the Church are not at all inconceivable. History shows us often enough that, whether in restricted or broader areas, leadership, forbearance, or legislation will, sooner or later, be shown to be largely inappropriate or erroneous.[6]

The same theologian adds, "The Church is a field filled with cockle, and not only among the ordinary faithful. In its pastoral government as well, the Spirit of God is not simply by itself, acting efficaciously; mediocrity, fallibility, and human weakness all make themselves felt in it." [7]

On behalf of churchmen of the past (and while remembering that God alone can probe the mind and the heart and measure the culpability of each of us), let us say that there have been progressive stages of awareness and that the problem of Christian politics has presented itself to Christians in quite varied historicosociological terms. Our purpose is not to know if, or in what degree, their behavior may be found excusable or explainable but to determine what are the ideal political demands on the Christian and what are objective errors in relationship to them. We have sketched out an analysis of the past only in order to try to clarify the causes and modalities of the evolution and deviation of practice, and thus to see more clearly what we should think and do today.

Is it really necessary after Vatican II to apologize for recalling that everything has not necessarily been for the best in the Church and for maintaining that it is not illicit, much

[6] Joseph Jungmann, *L'Annonce de la foi* (1965), pp. 28–29.

[7] *Ibid.*, pp. 98–99. The author also adds as a footnote a statement by Yves Congar: "Before the tendency, which sometimes manifests itself, of seeing in the Church nothing but the divine element and recognizing failings only in the private sphere of its representatives, we have also spoken here of the inclination to monophysitism, in terms of which the human element in the person of Jesus Christ is largely ignored" (*Le Christ, Marie, et l'Église* [1952], pp. 76 ff.).

less a sacrilege, to analyze the reasons for our past infidelities, if it is done in a constructive spirit?

Medieval Evangelism

Fortunately, the political achievement of the medieval Church was not limited to these grievous errors.

There was, first, the permanent establishment and even the growth of what we have called aid to humanity, an effect of the secondary action of the Church, its substitute function, which follows implicitly from various points of doctrine. In this way, for example, the elevation of woman, which began in the very first centuries of the Church, was intensified, thanks particularly to a spiritualization of love; in certain areas—Germany and England, for example—the number of convents for women was septupled in three centuries (from the tenth to the thirteenth centuries). There was also a greater dignity given (which was relatively just as important) to humble folk, simple rustics, and countrymen, on whom the Church depended and to whom it opened its doors and monasteries through the institution of the lay brother.

Both the truce of God and the sanctifying of chivalry were efforts to limit the warrior's violence and bring it to an end; many institutions, as ingenious as efficacious, responded to the needs of the sick and the development of culture. Arts, sciences, and letters attained a grandeur in the Middle Ages that even today does not cease to amaze us.

The age of the cathedrals was also that of the summas. In these impressive philosophical and theological constructions, the search for political implications in the Gospel was not absent. Alongside the censor bearers of imperial or pontifical absolutism, some doctors elaborated a more subtle position, as would be evident, for example, in a close examination of Saint Thomas' *On the Government of Princes*. Precursors, and geniuses are also to be found, such as John of Paris, theoretician of the separation of Church and State at the very zenith of the Middle Ages. But such a study would go beyond the framework of this hasty historical sketch.[8]

Most important, the Middle Ages has, to its own honor, also borne witness to very noble realizations of evangelical politics. In the face of a powerful and feudal Church, which was sometimes oppressive to the poor, the Waldensians preached by word and example a return to the Gospel, but they fell back into an obvious antievangelism through their refusal, ultimately, of any political incarnation. Nevertheless, without leaving the Church, some men began to become conscious of the need for evangelical renewal, and we can invoke in this connection the great names of Francis of Assisi and Dominic of Osma. We know—the very name of the mendicant orders is a sufficient indication in itself—the concern for total poverty preached by both these founders, not simply a spiritual poverty of the individual that would permit the development of wealthy religious communities but a material poverty that would require both Franciscans and Dominicans to depend for their daily bread on the charity of the faithful. Indeed, this total and spectacular poverty brought Francis, by experiencing the wounds of the crucified Lord, to "the perfect joy" promised by Jesus to those who are persecuted for his sake. This joy is the common good of a redeemed world in which men

[8] We must also emphasize the authentic evangelical inspiration that lay behind the political thought and action of Saint Catherine of Siena. See her letters especially, including one she wrote to a cardinal who had taken a city by storm at the head of the papal armies, in which she spoke of "mad wolves" and "devils incarnate."

no longer act as wolves to each other, and the animate and inanimate beings of all creation sing together in rediscovery of a primitive symphony.

Poverty was also vigorously felt by Saint Dominic. Even before founding his order, did he not advise the papal legates who were working among the Albigensians to abandon their seignorial train, a source of scandal to the Catharis, and did he not also preach by example? Did he not establish his convents in the strictest poverty, with the exception, it is true, of books, but books were needed to pursue heretics in the field of philosophical and theological disputation?

We know all this, and it has all been said before. But it is less generally said, except in specialized circles, that by this action the Church found itself in agreement with the rising concern for communal liberties in reaction against the feudalism of secular lords and both regular and secular clergy, a movement that it thereby upheld, encouraging the growth of the middle classes against those who held power.

Besides, these new disciples of Christ, having broken with the existing theological structures, quite naturally came to rediscover the true meaning of the internationalism of evangelical preaching and set out in every area, from Scandinavia to Tartary and Morocco, on missions in which for the first time since Charlemagne evangelization was not subordinate to conquest by arms.

The Growth of Nationalism

From the inextricable complexity of the Middle Ages, which mixed night and day, the most unfortunate bequest to modern times was certainly its forgetting of that sovereign indifference Jesus had professed in regard to the "formal" aspect of political power.

Whereas the Church should lead the men of all races and

cultures to supernatural salvation, it became in fact linked to a particular civilization. Regalists and papalists stubbornly sought to realize a symbiosis of Church and State. If they were in opposition as to the unifying pole of this whole, they were fundamentally in agreement. The result too frequently was a real political disincarnation of Christians in those fields in which the Gospel had sowed such rich seed.

In 1438 *La Pragmatique Sanction* assigned the nomination of bishops to the king of France, and in fact, the inheritance of the Concordat of Bologna, even up to the French Revolution, was a long line of "Gallican" bishops, of which Bossuet was the most famous representative. Another unfortunate result of this arrangement was that the great monasteries, which formerly had been centers of culture and holiness, were handed over to nonresident superiors, often of a worldly and unedifying disposition, "court abbés," who were responsible for the deplorable decadence in monastic life; this was one of the blemishes of the Gallican Church.

Luther, for his part, stirred up the fires of German nationalism and even announced : "We cannot refuse the title of priest and bishop to the prince, nor the privilege of considering his burden as a spiritual function, one that is Christian and useful to the entire community. . . ." This was the theorem that one of this disciples, Capito, was to specify in these terms: "The prince is a pastor, a father, the visible leader of the Church on earth. Christ has given to pious princes the gift of governing by conferring on them the prudence needed to govern piously. That is why he has wished that each prince be the leader of each of his churches in the world." Such a proposition, in its turn, led Luther—like all his Christian predecessors and successors, Roman or non-Roman—to betray the Gospel equally on the level of real politics (hence, ultimately, on the spiritual level), and to write, for example, to the German princes, after the bloody peasant rebellion had been repressed in the name of the Gospel: "Dear Lords, deliver us, come to our aid. Slash out, slaughter as many as you can. . . . An anarchist does not deserve to be given reasons by us, because he will not accept them. People like that should be answered with a good punch! . . . The ass wants to receive blows and the people want to be governed by force. God knows this well, for He has not given governors a fox's tail, but a bayonet!"

Nationalism, blood, money,[9] power: these are the consequences of the abandonment of the political doctrine of the Gospel. This can be verified in both camps. In the Spain of Charles V, the Inquisition, like all the works of the emperors, began as theocratic and shortly became casesaropapist. Sixtus V knew this well when he wrote in 1589 to his legate in France: "The conservation of the Catholic religion, which is the principal purpose of the pope, is only a pretext for His Majesty. This is because his principal purpose is the security and growth of the State."

The scenery for the drama had been solidly built; from now on it was to be well understood that *cuius regio, eius religio*, that religion was the business of the prince. There can no longer be any complaint about men fighting each other and killing each other. All the wars of this time, including international wars, found their cause in the Chris-

[9] On the significance of the love of money in Church history, we should remind ourselves that the occasion for the Lutheran protest was furnished by the dissatisfaction aroused in Germany by the means (including the sale of indulgences) used by the papacy to obtain funds.

In addition, the Reformers, abandoning the condemnation of lending money at interest, which had been the position of medieval theologians, came to terms with—and, according to some historians, even encouraged—the growth of modern capitalism (to which, of course, Catholic theologians also ended up accommodating themselves). See Gatheron, *L'Usure dévorante*.

tian religion, or at least their occasion, or their pretext. This betrayal of evangelical politics will always be a source of scandal. What became of the commandment of Love?

When only such a faint voice is raised on behalf of peace, the whole human order is poisoned at its source. It is only natural that later history witnessed revolutions proclaimed in the name of deceptive rivalries between the remains of papal theocratic pretension and various forms of caesaropapism, as well as among these caesaropapisms themselves, and also among the Protestant princes and Catholic princes.

8

BOSSUET, VICTIM OF
HIS CENTURY

Before proceeding to the chapter on revolutions, we might well stop a moment to look more attentively at a monument of the *ancien régime* Catholic mentality—the treatise of Bossuet, whose title and design are so close to our own: *La Politique tirée des propres paroles de l'Écriture sainte.*

Although contaminated by the confusions of its environment, this work is more deserving than its period. Traces of caesaropapism and theocracy are certainly evident in it, especially when the Eagle of Meaux defends the divine right of kings and, forgetting the special, theological status of the Jewish people, wants to base his *Politique* on the practice of the people of Israel, as if they could be used as a prototype for other peoples. In addition, the work suffers from a disequilibrium in its use of scripture; it is remarkable that Bossuet drew almost exclusively on the Old Testament. Indeed, he himself was forced to become aware of this, for the twelfth proposition of Book II—that is, the very last page of this huge volume—is entitled "Special Reflection on the Situation of Christianity." No doubt he wanted to compose for the Dauphin a treatise on politics that would be as technically complete as possible but was himself uneasy when he realized how few of his political texts were from the Gospels; of course, this should have been a warning to him that the real political values of the Gospel would have to be sought elsewhere. In spite of everything, however, and thanks to both his knowledge of scripture and a certain sensitivity to the Gospel that secretly tormented him, Bossuet retained some profoundly evangelical intuitions, astonishing for his time. But the good seed is curiously mixed with the bad.

The two tendencies are apparent in the preamble to Monseigneur le Dauphin; it begins badly, in the finest blend of theocratic confusion and misunderstanding of the privileged destiny of Israel:

God is the King of kings: it is for Him to instruct them and govern them as His ministers. Listen, then, my Lord, to the lessons that He gives them in scripture. . . . We see here the government of a people of whom God Himself was the legislator.

All that Sparta, all that Athens, all that Rome, and to return to the source, all that Egypt and all well-governed states have contained that was most wise is nothing in comparison with the wisdom that is enclosed in the law of God, from which other laws have drawn that which was best in them.

There has also never been a finer constitution for a state than that possessed by the people of God.

But the end of the preamble is better; it can and should be understood in the sense of a real incarnation of the political principles of Christ:

Jesus Christ will teach us, either himself or through his apostles, everything that serves to make states happy. His Gospel leads men to be better equipped to be good citizens on earth, just as it also teaches them by this means to make themselves worthy of becoming citizens of Heaven.

God, finally, through whom kings hold their rule, leaves out nothing needed to teach them to rule well. The ministers of princes, and those who have a share under their authority in the government of states and the administration of its justice, will find lessons in His word that God alone was able to give. It is part of Christian morality to form magistrates by a training in its laws. God has wished to decide everything—that is, to give decisions to all ranks of society, and most especially to the one on whom all others depend.

This, my Lord, is the greatest of all purposes that can be proposed to men, who could never be too attentive to the rules by which they will be judged with an eternal and irrevocable sentence. Those who believe that piety implies an enfeebling of politics will be confounded, and the politics you will behold is truly divine.

In effect, Book I "On the Principles of Society Among Men," shows a rare and acute sense of genuine evangelical politics. Article 1 argues that "man is made to live in society," and this is not based on a philosophical principle, but on scripture, and what is more, for once, on the Gospel. The first proposition reminds us of the principle "Seek ye first the Kingdom of God." ("Men have only one and the same end and object, which is God"). The second proposition, "The love of God obliges men to love each other," is based on Mark 12:29–31 and Matthew 22:40; the third uses Matthew 23:8–9 in order to affirm that "All men are brothers"; the fourth is based on the parable of the Good Samaritan; the fifth specifies that "Each man should be concerned for other men," and so on. We see that Bossuet had certainly grasped several key points of the profoundly political incarnation of the Gospel.

After having evoked the birth and division of society in articles 2–4, Bossuet, in the one proposition of article 5 of the same book, declared, "The sharing of goods among men and the very division of men into peoples and nations should not alter the general society of human kind in any way." In other words, Bossuet was quite aware of the anti-evangelical dangers inherent in property and nationalism.

But everything goes wrong from the beginning of Book II almost up to the end of the volume (Book X). This can be seen precisely at the point that the bishop of Meaux treats of monarchy, thereby involuntarily bringing one more proof of our affirmation that in deviating from the evangelical position on "formal" politics, one also abandons the most original contribution of the Gospel to "real" politics. In fact, Book II, in dealing with authority, affirms that "royal and hereditary authority is most fitting for government"; we are forced to wonder what verse of the Gospel was Bossuet's source for this certainty. Of course, what he would say is that it is not in the Gospel but in the Old Testament, for in Book III, "where we begin to explain the nature and characteristics of royal authority," he constantly makes use of the parallel with Israel in order to demonstrate such principles as "Royal authority is sacred," "God established kings as His ministers and governs His people through them," "The person of kings is sacred," and "Men should obey the prince as a principle of religion and conscience."

As against this, we have already seen the sophistry resulting from the fact that the sacred destiny of Israel is ignored. There is, accordingly, no reason to be surprised to see both the best and the worst emerge from the argumentation of the Eagle of Meaux. We just enumerated the caesaropapist theses (Book III article 2); in the sequel (article 3), while making excessive use of the Old Testament texts,[1] Bossuet nevertheless wrote some better "propositions," perhaps because he found himself on the solid terrain of what had not changed from the Old to the New Testament:

The royal authority is paternal, and its proper character is goodness. . . . Goodness is a royal quality. . . . The prince is

[1] For example, "The Lord said to David: You will shepherd my people Israel. Hence, it is not only Homer who calls princes the pastors of nations, but also the Holy Spirit."

not born for himself but for the public. . . . The prince ought to provide for the needs of his people . . . be among them as one of them. . . . Take care of them and take your rest only after providing for everything. . . . Among the people, those to whom the prince should most provide are the feeble. . . . The true character of the prince is to provide for the needs of his people, just as that of the tyrant is to think only of himself. . . . A good prince spares human blood and detests any action that involves the shedding of blood. . . . Government ought to be gentle. . . .

But the fourth and following books revert to the most inacceptable confusion. We need refer only to a few examples: "Royal authority is absolute" (VI, 1), "The prince should use his authority to eliminate all false religions in his state," and "It is permissible to employ rigorous means against those who practice false religions, but mild methods are preferable" (VII, 9, 10). Book VIII, which is consecrated to justice, includes a particularly significant proposition:

The private ownership of goods is legitimate and inviolable. We have seen the distribution of lands under Joshua, according to the orders of Moses (Joshua 13, 14, ff.); it was the way to bring them into cultivation, and experience shows that land that is held in common or simply without a legitimate and irremovable owner, is neglected and abandoned. That is why it is not permitted to abandon this order [VIII, 2].

In other words, in order to establish the idea of private property on a religious basis, Bossuet was reduced to referring to the book of Joshua; he ended up by stressing common experience, which runs counter to the claim of his volume that it is a politics drawn from Holy Scripture (*La Politique tirée de l'Écriture sainte*).

The last two books (IX and X) are equally filled with implicit contradictions of Gospel imperatives. Book IX, dealing with "the services of the royalty," is not limited to presenting the theory of the just war; after having eliminated the "unjust motives of war" (article 2), Bossuet gave war God's guarantee, always in the name of Israel: "God raises up warrior princes. . . . God gave the Israelites the explicit commandment to wage war" (article 1, first and second propositions). The question of conscientious objection is handled in the same way: "They proceeded by arms to punish those who did not enter the army, because the commandment had been given by a public order" (article 3, third proposition); the example cited in this case was that of Gideon (Jug 8:16 ff.).

"The services of the royalty" were continued in the tenth and final book, along with wealth and finances. In the very first proposition of article 1, a man might well be struck by the evangelical spirit of the thesis: "There are expenses for necessities; there are also those called for by the claims of splendor and dignity." But suddenly Saint Paul comes to the rescue, quoted in obvious contradiction of his real meaning: "Who serves as a soldier at his own expense?" (1 Co 9:7).

After such accommodations, the work is well prepared for its conclusion—on the beatitude of the poor, as long as the approach to the subject has now shifted to the method of spiritual exegesis!

And yet, does not Bossuet deserve more respect than that? His *Politique* was doubly restricted: first, by its recipient, the Dauphin; second, by the accepted ideas of the time. But did he not preserve a certain evangelical awareness? We have already seen sporadic indications of this; there are others in the remainder of his work.

Fundamentally, the explanation of these fluctuations does not rest in the fact that—as one sometimes has the impression—Bossuet did not dare to follow his intuitions and his arguments to their logical end. When we find him in meditation before the crib at Bethlehem, he seems to understand that the Christmas story itself condemns the world and the pursuit of wealth: "Ah, if we could only leave everything!"

Christians, do not think that you can approach this throne of poverty still weighed down with your love of wealth and grandeur. Stop deceiving yourselves, and give up your illusions; you who come to the crib of Our Lord, deprive yourselves, at least in spirit. *Would that we had the courage really to give up everything, in order to follow as poor men the king of the poor!* Let us at least give up everything in spirit, and instead of glorifying in the display of wealth that surrounds us, let us be ashamed to be adorned while Jesus Christ was born naked and destitute [sixteenth week, sixth elevation].

Who would have suspected it? Bossuet was a tortured man, consumed with anxiety, and it was the Gospel that created this tension in him.

It is thus that his *Traité de l'usure* is completely in keeping with the evangelical demands regarding loans and gifts, as is seen in a brief analysis:

First proposition: "In the old law usury was forbidden from brother to brother, that is, among Israelites. . . ."

Second proposition: "The spirit of the law is to forbid usury because it contains something evil in itself."

Third proposition: "Christians have always believed that this law against usury was obligatory according to the Gospel."

Fourth proposition: "Not only is the prohibition of usury maintained in the old law still in force, but it was to be perfected in the new law, according to the constant spirit of the evangelical precepts."

Fifth proposition: "The doctrine that says that usury, according to the idea of it already given, is forbidden in the new law to all men and between all men is a matter of faith."

Sixth proposition: "The contrary opinion is without foundation."

Seventh proposition: "The law of God forbidding usury at the same time forbids all practices equivalent to it."

Eighth proposition: "The ecclesiastical and civil police, in order to prevent the effect of usury, should use great rigor not only to prevent what is usury but also to prevent everything that leads to it."

We have included this extensive analysis of Bossuet because of his place in history at the conclusion of theocratic and caesaropapist errors and also because of his attempt, which has rarely been made in the history of Christian thought, to work out a politics drawn from Holy Scripture. But we see that, in spite of some occasional insights that were quite accurate, his overall design was vitiated by the caesaropapist confusion that leads to grave betrayals when it is a question of real politics, especially in anything that involves money, violence, and justice. Still, Bossuet's effort is one of the most nuanced and faithful efforts to work within this framework. It is from this confused situation that modern revolutions derive; in them we see its disastrous consequences.

9

CENTURIES OF REVOLUTION

The Agony of Caesaropapism

In July 1790, scarcely a year after the convocations of the States-General and the capture of the Bastille, when euphoria still reigned, a Gallican demopapism took over from Gallican caesaropapism. In all good faith, without wanting to be or thinking of themselves as schismatic, the majority of the National Assembly passed the decree that established the civil constitution of the clergy; ecclesiastics of every rank, instead of being appointed by the king or by their superiors, would be chosen by citizens of the department concerned; none of them would ask for the spiritual investiture by the pope; a bishop who had already taken up his functions should inform the pope, but simply out of courtesy.

It should come as no surprise to us that Gallicans could invent and accept such a regime. In their eyes, power, instead of being incarnate in the king, was now established in the people; the problem was civil, not religious.

Nevertheless, in the course of time the civil constitution

of the clergy became an apple of discord in French Catholicism and a cause of rupture between the Republic and the Church. It would be too lengthy and delicate a task to try to set down here why this happened. All the motivations involved in the controversy were not equally pure. The clergy was called upon to abandon "the goods of the Church" to the State and to take the risk of returning to their original evangelical poverty, but an ideological opposition also became evident and was to last for a long time. In fact, although many priests and bishops were sincerely won over to the new situations and the political philosophy of the day, others continued to think, like Bossuet, that "royal authority is sacred." [1]

The latter began to look for and to find heresies in the Declaration of the Rights of Man and of the Citizen, which had nevertheless been able to win support from the bishops in the Assembly. In his brief, *Quod aliquantulum*, of March 10, 1791, Pius VI spoke of the "extravagant liberty" of its constituents.

During almost all the nineteenth century the majority of the French clergy came to adopt this opposition to republican ideas and to drag the Church over the long and unhappy road of "reaction," thereby making it incapable of grasping what was not only reasonable but even a transposition of the Gospel, on the civil level, in the words "liberty," "justice," and "fraternity."

In the same way, the Church for a long time also preserved its nostalgia for "the very Christian king," the "a-

---

[1] Obviously, the opposition of a part of the clergy to the civil constitution also had more fundamental doctrinal reasons, especially after the pope had spoken. It should also be recognized that the revolution became more and more anti-Christian—but was not this evolution due in great part to the abstention and later to the resistance on the part of the hierarchy, for in its beginnings the renewal had been animated by a religious thought that unhappily became more ephemeral and heretical?

nointed of the Lord," [2] identified in turn as Napoleon I,
Charles X, Napoleon III—and the Count de Chambord!
Even at the dawn of the twentieth century, some religious
were still circulating prophecies and private "revelations"
proclaiming the imminent coming of the "great pope" and
"the great king."

"Liberal Catholicism," deriving from Lamennais and the
"social Catholicism" of the nineteenth and twentieth centuries, also retained a certain nostalgia for the Catholic State,
as was seen in their assumptions regarding Christian democracy [3]; meanwhile the integralists still dreamed of caesaropapism or a pontifical monarchy, conceived in the manner
of Innocent III or Boniface VII.

The encyclical *Immortale Dei*, released in 1878 by Leo
XIII, produced no real effect. Nevertheless, in recalling
that civil society and religious society—one concerned with
the temporal order, the other with the spiritual—"are each
sovereign in their sphere," it was only returning to the
Gospel. When, in 1892, the same pope addressed another
encyclical especially to French Catholics to summon them
back to religious indifference in regard to the type of political regime adopted in a particular country and to advise
them to "rally" to the Republic, to accept its constitution
in order to make improvements in its legislation, his direc-
tives were in general very badly received, both by clericalists and by anticlericals. Both looked with scorn on Leo's
action as nothing but cleverness and the calculated maneu-
vering of an opportunistic diplomacy. The fact is that if
Catholics had stopped their bitter internal struggles on behalf of positions relating to "formal" politics, they would

[2] This is how the "imperial catechism" described Napoleon.

[3] Certain movements should be cited as exceptions because
their efforts were in the realm of real politics, with little concern
as to the kind of government under which social justice was to be
pursued—Léon Harmel, the Équipes sociales, for example.

have been able to work more effectively to put the Gospel into practice in the world of "real" politics.

We must say in their defense that the other side also continued to argue in terms of an indefensible caesaropapism. It is known, but rarely mentioned, that the separation of Church and State was held up for a long time because certain leading politicians, although themselves anticlerical, found it convenient to exercise a hold over the clergy by the device of the designation of bishops and that the extremists themselves, including Combes, who finally achieved his victory with the law of December 9, 1905, at the same time nourished the avowed design of establishing a kind of schism (the most recent history of communist countries has furnished us with other examples in the same style). The result was that the separation of Church and State in France—with its great influence on the response of Catholics in other countries to the same issues—which should have been welcomed with enthusiasm by Christians as an opportunity to return to the Gospel, was accepted by them at best as a lesser evil and with great misgivings.

From Proudhon to Maritain

In the intellectual domain, too, the old confusions persisted for a long time, even among the most revolutionary. Here again we can only pick out a few examples.

Proudhon, for instance, placed revolution and Church in opposition, seeing the latter only as "favoritism, and arbitrary and illicit meddling of the clergy in everyday life, an illegitimate growth of ecclesiastical property, a danger for families and free labor"—in brief, "a profound immorality." [4]

[4] *De la justice dans la Révolution et dans l'Église: Nouveaux principes de philosophie politique* (1859), I, 519. The author had

Saint-Simon, having reread the Gospels, was more sensitive—as we see in *Le Nouveau Christianisme* (1825)—to what the law of love in the Sermon on the Mount might imply as consequences in the domain of politics. Unfortunately, because he was as obsessed as the Romantics by the Middle Ages and also confused genuine political incarnation and formal political incarnation, he wanted to reestablish a power as sovereign as the medieval papacy was, in order to create a society as classless as medieval society was (according to him); in other words, the Church had disappointed him, so he wanted to found a new one.

Buchez, his disciple, founder of the journal *L'Atelier*, who was the leader of the Christian socialists and had been converted after having read and reread *Le Nouveau Christianisme*,[5] tried in vain to persuade the Saint-Simonians, as well as official Catholicism, that it was not a question of founding a new religion but of re-evangelizing the sociology and politics of Christianity. He showed that the positive contribution of the Church in the political domain is to be measured by its fidelity to the Gospel and its incarnation at the level of what we have called real politics: the equality of sexes, classes, and races is an evolutionary transposition of the equality of the faithful before the mystery of Christ and his sacraments. The same is true in regard to the unity of mankind, and its expansion to new areas should be seen as a sign of the unity of the mystical body.

For Buchez, everything that had been accomplished that was good and constructive in the course of history was due to the ferment of the Gospel: the emancipation of the serfs, bourgeois, and artisans, the promotion of the third estate,

ironically addressed his work to the Archbishop of Besançon and all the clergy of France.

[5] This led him to the Gospel but not to the frequentation of the sacraments. Until the eve of his death in 1865—as his legal executor, Frederic Ott, put it—he was to remain "on the threshold of the Church of which he was only the concierge.

community privileges, and so on; everything bad was the result of neopagan infiltration: absolute monarchy, caesarism, and so on. In the last analysis, if the revolution was anticlerical and antireligious, it was because a defaulting clergy and nobility were anti-Christian. Thus he concluded, in opposition to Proudhon (*L'Atelier*, September 1, 1840): "If the laity want to take the trouble to examine finally without prejudice the movement of ideas, they will immediately be able to measure the power that Christian dogma can provide, even to minds as little cultivated as our own. They would then realize that Christianity and revolution are one and the same thing and that the only fault of the Church is not being revolutionary."

On the level of philosophical reflection applied to politics, a man of our own time, Jacques Maritain, has played a decisive role. We cannot forget what he accomplished by example, with a sure evangelical sensitivity, at the moment of the crisis of Action française and later by the stands he took against the Spanish civil war and the pagan racism of Hitler's Germany. Since *The Things That Are Not Caesar's* and *True Humanism*, Maritain's complete work shows that he has never ceased to be preoccupied with the problems of Christian politics. Coming himself from a republican family, he later became sympathetic with Action française due to religious obedience (and to such unfortunate advisers as Père Clérissac and Dom Delatte) and thus found himself deeply involved in the absurdity of caesaropapist confusion and in the world of formal politics. The truth is that he had a great deal of difficulty in extricating himself from this morass, but in doing so, he also liberated a great many others and, by this act, earned great merit from the Church. In addition, his formation and taste for philosophical speculation made him more inclined to develop a long chain of reasoning on abstract ideas and on the heritage left by metaphysicians and moralists than to draw conclusions directly from the Word of God. That is why, along with his excellent studies, which ultimately link up with the evangelical spirit—for example, on freedom, education, and justice—he spent a great deal of time in overcoming the religious pseudoproblem of democracy and in recognizing that, far from it being opposed to Christianity, it contained, virtually, some important Christian values. Besides, by inventing the celebrated distinction between the action of the Christian in the city *en chrétien* and *en tant que chrétien*—between acting as a Christian and acting as a representative of the Church—he managed, contrary to his intentions, to furnish a dangerous alibi with which Christians who are not really interested in incarnating the commands of Christ in the whole area of politics were glad to cover themselves. This distinction—between someone acting in a Christian spirit and someone working with an officially Christian organization—should not have led him to be so easily resigned to see Christians opposing each other on a particular essential political problem that was really fundamental and ought to be resolved by a pure and simple obedience to the teaching of Christ itself. The "primacy of the spiritual" would fall into angelism (rightly denounced by the philosopher of Meudon) if it tranquilized Christians who still hesitate to become involved in politics and priests who take refuge in the comfort of a prudent neutralism.

III
TODAY

10

SIGNS OF THE TIMES

It is as a consequence neither of a theoretical reflection nor of the fruitless and dangerous maneuvers of the Church in the area of formal politics that today's return to a political incarnation of Christians in a more evangelical sense has become visible. As it had been prescribed by the Lord, the key factor was an interior deepening, a very simple but fervent search for the Kingdom of God and his justice. The main advocates of this development, as well as most of those especially active in it, would themselves be astonished if they were told that they were—and are—in the process of realizing a genuine Christian politics. Nevertheless, this is the case. The fact is that almost all these Christians were and are animated by a rediscovery of the Gospel, with all its demands for incarnation.

Nevertheless, a faith that has been made more responsive to the Gospel is immediately forced to see most cruelly its total absence from the modern world. This helps to explain the shock of *France Pagan?* in which Abbé Godin rediscovered the necessity of simply carrying the Gospel, as in mission countries, to the so-called civilized nations. It resulted in various efforts at the internal renewal of Church in an evangelical sense, a movement that tended to be in opposition to an accommodation with the spirit of the world and its institutions. The double maneuver of detachment from the "world" (in the evangelical sense of everything that is not simply Jesus crucified) and of commitment or incarnation in the world (in the sense of nature) is characteristic of all the movements of thought and action that have developed out of modern evangelism—the workerpriests, the Little Brothers of Jesus, the social theology of Père Chenu, the Jesuits of Action populaire, the Economie et Humanisme group, and so on. Again we encounter the typical tensions and resolutions of the Gospel. That is why these modern apostles and their guides are so much at ease in the Gospel. The Gospel, writes Father Loew in *Mission to the Poorest,*

shows itself every day as a genuine rule of life, more adapted, more precise, and far more liberating than a religious constitution or a book of common law. Basically, what the people ask for from the Church is the Gospel, and from the priest they are looking for the evangelical life. Instead, when they go to the Church, they see candles, statues, and ornaments, but where would they be able to find the Gospel? But the Gospel is love. Love is no longer loved, it is no longer held in esteem.[1]

The revival of Biblical studies encouraged many to take up the Holy Scriptures directly for themselves as rules for life and action; the Young Christian Workers and their study circles constantly spoke of trying to put "The Gospel in our lives." Ecumenism, besides encouraging a

[1] Jacques Loew, O.P., *Mission to the Poorest* (1950), end of Chapter 4 and Chapter 7. See also at the end of Chapter 4: "Vivified by the Gospel and poverty, material and moral assistance has a fullness of efficacity." See also, at the beginning of Chapter 5, in speaking of a mass said in a plain room and in ordinary clothes, "Whether one likes it or not, how close we all felt to the Lord Jesus of the Gospel!"

benevolent osmosis, also served to eliminate service to any state religion. The various movements of the workers' section of Catholic action began to recognize, on one hand, that the life of faith, its witness and the possibility of its diffusion, implied a total independence from any formal political structure and, on the other hand, that nothing in their faith was foreign to their day-to-day life and their struggles in society, and vice versa. They discovered, therefore, little by little, after meeting with setbacks and making mistakes, the difficult necessity of a faith that would be simultaneously disengaged and engaged, spiritual and incarnate, free from every compromise and obedient in every detail to the concrete precepts of Christ. A part of the clergy suddenly became aware of this recovered freedom that should never have been lost; if they remained truly *segregatus*, chosen, set apart, it was *in Evangelium*, on behalf of the Gospel, for the purpose of preaching the Good News and not in order to be a social class among other classes. Leaving this heritage far behind them, abandoning this last stone witness of theocratic and caesaropapist systems, they can be seen integrating themsleves with the real political life of the country, as workers, peasants, engineers, employees, and ragpickers. As a result of all this, we began to notice these Christians, both priests and laymen, discovering and adopting, in unanimity, some real political decisions regarding freedom, money, and justice. In addition, who will be able to measure the political effectiveness, whether immediately or from a long term point of view, of these parishes in the suburbs, in slums, in workers' quarters, in which the Gospel, preached in all its practical force within the Church, is realized outside it, without rhetoric or pretension but in fervor and truth? Here are centers where fraternal love is an everyday reality, where the worries, the joys, and the children of one family are also those of others; concern for money and internal dissensions have been transcended,

along with sterile and superficial arguments. Instead, people
are grappling with the real world, its injustices and miseries.
The Church has been made poor—that is, it has been partly
returned to its congenital and true state of meager
resources—and now provides the good soil where, in spite
of attacks and the efforts of those who sow cockle, a part
of that good grain can spring up, grow to maturity, and
come to fruition.

All this and many other efforts of the same character explain how the contemporary Church, confronted with situations that are apparently quite "political"—that is, simply
quite visible and external—has reacted in a way that had
not been seen since the time of the first Christians.

We have a number of recent examples of this. In March
1966 there was a widely noted declaration, solidly con-
structed and clearly expressed, that, in spite of embarrassed
explanations of some politically minded functionaries, was
a sharp attack on the profit economy and liberal capitalism.
Somewhat earlier, at the risk of displeasing the Chief of
State, during a strike of miners in 1963 French bishops took
political positions that did not conform with those of the
government.

An even more decisive example should be pointed out in
connection with the tragic war in Algeria, which was the
occasion of many atrocities, and so many instances of torture. This was perhaps the first time since Christ that a
Church almost unanimous in its principal elements—both
the hierarchy and active laymen—calmly stood up, without
provocation or disturbance, against the established power,
in the face of a fundamental action of its own country, in
order to say "No." This "No" was explicitly offered as a
judgment against the tortures, violence, and civil war, and
it was quite widely known that the organization of resistance to subversion and perversion in the contingent were

often furnished by seminarians and Christian activists. Indeed, the refusal also concerned, in a manner scarcely more veiled, the continuation of the Algerian war itself. All this occurred to the great astonishment and scandal of the vast majority of officers and of some free-lance priests and laymen who thought of themselves as battling for the true faith. Undoubtedly, most of the opposition was to this unjust war rather than to war in itself; but besides the fact that it is not irrelevant to the realization of the Gospel that Christians should be anxious about the liberty of others and the halting of all constraint, it is undeniable that a rejection of war itself has begun and that such a position can now be vaguely seen on the horizons of men's minds. The road covered since World War I, and even since the liberation movements of World War II, can easily be measured. In both cases, Christians rushed into combat, adding to the overall spirit of nationalism, as well as showing that their faith had not made them eunuchs. Benedict XV was called the Boche Pope by good Catholics simply because in 1915 he called on the belligerents to make peace in the name of God. Indeed, in the aftermath of both these terrible wars, one could see Christians, both priests and laymen, more proud of their victory than of their faith, setting up various veterans' organizations, congratulating each other that the warm atmosphere of the front lines had been so helpful for making converts, and calling for the blood of enemies or collaborators. In such a situation the evangelical veto of war, violence, and judgment was completely forgotten, as if any acts of revenge could redeem crimes as atrocious as those of national socialism, much less suppress their causes. We can see, then, that in this area Christians have made some progress; this is understood even more clearly when we recall that, little by little abandoning those vain scholastic discussions on the question of a just war, which had been sterile since the Middle Ages and the Jesuit and

Dominican theologians of the Counter Reformation, Christian thought has begun to familiarize itself with the complete prohibition of all war. *"Bellum est omnino interdicendum,"* wrote Cardinal Ottaviani, who could hardly be considered suspect for modernism.

Other practical applications of the evangelical spirit that are openly social and political have recently marked the political mutation of the Church. Not content with promoting, by the example of its own organization and the encouragement of words, the independence of poor nations that had been under colonial domination until recently, the Church has tried to arouse a profound movement of fraternal assistance for peoples whose economic development has been inadequate and to encourage international cooperation and unification in peace and justice.

The definitive sign of this mutation that is beginning to take place was furnished by the good Pope John—both the man and his work. If his life and death awakened such an affectionate interest throughout the world, in all circles of life, in all classes and races, it is quite simply because he knew how to rediscover both the substance and the accents of the Gospel of Christ. In fact, as much by himself as by the council that he called together, he signified clearly to the world that the Christian faith ought, on behalf of and by means of Christians, to inform all economic, social, and political realities. At the same time, through all sorts of means (such as the general tone of his encyclicals and his life, his meeting with Adzhubei, the son-in-law of Khrushchev, despite the proximity of Italian elections), he showed no less clearly a firm determination to reject any form of theocracy; even better, he completely ignored this idea, as if it had no meaning and had never existed. He gave his teaching to Christians as the point of departure for their doctrine and to others as an offer made from equal to equal, without any desire or hidden thought of domination but also without any hope of tactical concession. What pope was more involved in the political realities of the world and more removed from the spirit of submission to the world or domination over it? *Mater et magistra* and *Pacem in terris* are models of what should always have been the political action of the Church: "Here is what we think, here is what we want, here is what we Christians are going to try to do; do you agree with us? Can we do it together?" Thus, it is somewhat inaccurate to speak, in connection with the action of John XXIII, of an *aggiornamento*, that is, of an updating, a rejuvenation of the Church; it is much rather a return to the source, a resort to the Gospel in our very midst. And all this would not have been possible, as Pope John himself admitted, if it had not been prepared, pursued, and in some sense pleaded for by a whole mass of rediscoveries, individual research, personal testimony, and individual and collective efforts, a few of which we have mentioned and of which John XXIII, under the guidance of the Holy Spirit, was able to make himself the receiver, the collector, and the pilot.

This rapidly sketched outline of evangelical politics in our time could rightly be criticized for simplification and excessive optimism. The latter is intentional to the extent that we want to suggest that there is a tendency at work in groups that perhaps may still constitute a numerical minority but nevertheless represent the avant garde of the Church and even the direction that is officially being taken.

Obviously, there is no question of pretending that the whole Church is in this situation. We have not forgotten that the Spanish- and Portuguese-speaking countries, for example, are all too often still troubled with important effects of caesaropapism; nor have we forgotten the painful backward step imposed on the French worker-priests in 1954; nor the subterranean and unhappy action of irresponsible small groups, still nostalgic for past political errors—indeed, claiming them with pride, peevishness, and vanity—trying to establish secret cells among influential officials; nor the astonishing indifference of Christians; nor many other things. Although everything allows us to foresee the pointlessness of these various maneuvers, which at the most can constitute only an unfortunate rear-guard action, it is worthwhile at present to examine some of the points, that continue to create problems or that, having only recently been a source of division, weigh down the present situation with their own more or less dense shade and deeply effect the Christian mentality of our time, preventing or impeding a rapid and homogeneous action on the part of the Church in the domain of political evangelism.

In fact, today's Catholics continue to be divided on:

—The political order: monarchy or republic, or more precisely, monocracy or democracy

—The split between "rightist" and "leftist" mentalities

—Capitalism and socialism

What relationships do these disputes have with the demands of an evangelical politics? We would like to examine this question quickly, before concluding with recommendations for action.

11

MONOCRACY OR DEMOCRACY?

There is no need to repeat here what we have already cataloged in the first part of this book on evangelical indifference to the authorities and in the second part on Christian infidelity to this principle, culminating in a situation in which Christian thought and political action were for centuries haunted by the obsession of the divine right of kings.

Naturally, this is not the place to present the historical, economic, political, or philosophic arguments on the comparative advantages and disadvantages of a monarchy and a republic. It is simply a question of disclosing how these different regimes conduct themselves, actually and in relation to evangelical politics.

Such a study is neither useless nor anachronistic. On one side, the followers of Action française and the modern movements that sprang from it show that there always exists a certain receptivity in some areas of the Christian community to the virus of absolute monarchy; besides, the examination of the motives of attraction and repulsion in regard to various political systems and the confrontation of

these motives with the evangelical ideal seem indispensable
ways of eliminating all these abcesses and avoiding new errors in various directions.

For or Against Monocracy

Men have forged—and periodically continue to polish—
a whole arsenal of apparently logical arguments to justify
monarchy from the Christian point of view; all these justi-
fications show the imprint of the theocratic crisis, whether
it is a matter of placing authority in opposition to liberty
and showing that authority comes from God or of pretending that God has provided an example for the temporal
state by constructing the world of nature and grace according to a pyramidal, hierarchical mode, of which He is the
fine point, the head. The rational basis of such argumentation is completely inadequate, for authority is not exclusive
of liberty; it can be concretized in other ways than in a
monarch; and it *always* comes from God (if the question is
considered theologically), not only when it is incarnated in
a single man, because every being, every good, every order,
and every power participate, in order to be what they are
and to the degree in which they *are*, in the source of all
being. All that is left is the argument of the archetype of
divine government, which we may accept in part, as long as
it is well understood that we are speaking of an analogical
application (in view of the fact that every theocracy is
condemned by the Gospel) and on condition that the divine plan is loyally followed. When this is done, we
quickly perceive that the matter is not so simple, for the
evangelical revelation, which is also a revolution, teaches us
precisely that God is our father and that we are His children and that Jesus, son of the father, has made himself our
brother, our fellow man, and that it was for this reason that
he forfeited his throne, as Saint Paul magnificently ex-

plained to the Philippians: "His state was divine, yet he did
not cling to his equality with God but emptied himself to
assume the condition of a slave, and became as men are"
(2:6–8). We are no longer slaves, therefore, but heirs of
the house of God, equal not only among ourselves but
from a certain point of view to God, who has made us
equal to Him; the Kingdom of God is within us, between
our hands, in our power; and it depends on us to make it
grow. It is also clear that God wishes to be loved and not
feared; this, too, is the divine plan, but is not adequately
translated into the analogical transposition of the monarchical order to pyramidal hierarchy.

Besides, if all these arguments leading to the divine right
of monarchy are so fragile, is the reason not that they only
represent a rational screen for unconscious motivations that
are far deeper and less justifiable? The Christian theoreti-
cians of monarchy do not seem to have taken the trouble to
analyze its subsoil in order to verify whether there might
be some incompatibility between it and Christian Revelation. If they had done so, they would have discovered that
the infrastructure of the monarchical idea is perhaps not as
attractive as its apparent superstructure.

After all, is not the origin of monarchy more or less
magical? In order to account for it, we would need to have
recourse to the combined insights of history, sociology,
ethnology, psychology of the unconscious and of the collective unconscious, psychoanalysis, and so on. But it can
hardly be doubted that there is masochism, idolatry, totem-
ism, and all sorts of obscure magic feelings in the fact of
choosing or accepting a man (and a line), of attributing a
superior essence to him, venerating him, entering collectively into trances at his visits, treating him as an emanation
of oneself (as part of the group) and at the same time as the
divinity, obeying his every nod, considering him a savior, a
protector, a father, a chief, bowing down before his por-

trait with veneration . . . All these manifestations, which we understand quite well and which hardly surprise us because we consider them part of our history and our intellectual museum, are nevertheless quite strange and of special interest if someone looks at them with a fresh eye and, with the naïveté of a child, asks "why."

We would like to see specialists in the already mentioned disciplines begin to study the origins and psychosociological nature of monarchy. But surely we would not be deceiving ourselves a great deal if we stated that monarchy, whether royal or imperial, is profoundly enrooted in the magical substructure of man. The monarch—whether he is called king, emperor, chief, duce, führer, caudillo, guide, premier, first secretary, or number 1 of the party—is the efficacious symbol of the power, glory, and strength of the group.[1] He is a sort of hero and demigod, a "pontiff," a bridge between man and divinity. Through him the man in the crowd feels he can enter the realm of the absolute himself and be venerated. In the symbol he admires himself, and thereby achieves a kind of narcissistic and masochistic self-idolatry, body and spirit. Man loves his body; he loves to glorify it, contemplate it, venerate it; he also likes to make himself suffer, to humiliate his body and subdue it: and all this is achieved by the monarch. As for the spirit, the king represents the living totem, the perpetuity of the race, and the assurance of its terrestrial eternity.

We are hardly trying to suggest that one's face should be veiled before the world of magic. It is part of man and perhaps even constitutes the rich soil from which flowers, trees, and religions emerge. Not one of the least errors of

[1] "The indivisible authority of the State is completely given over to the president by the people who have elected him, and no authority exists, neither ministerial, civil, military, nor judicial, that is not conferred by him" (General de Gaulle, at his press conference, January 31, 1964).

Comte and Marx is the belief in the possibility of an evolution of man to a world of exclusively rational relationships; their notion of man was someone who in every sense of the word is a being of reason. Nevertheless, it is also necessary that this infrarational, symbolic world, which we tried to sum up with the term "magical," be kept in its place. Should it prevail in the area of political organization, where, it would seem, reason ought to dominate? This is a question we shall leave to sages; there are arguments pro and con in regard to it. It is enough for us, in the framework of this essay, to point out the danger rooting both the political spirit and the religious spirit in the substratum of magic activity, because it would seem that this subsoil ought to be reserved to the latter. Otherwise, how would it be possible to avoid confusion, unfortunate graftings, bastard fruits, and half-breed races? If not impossible in justice, it would seem at least difficult in fact. History shows us this, examples not only of theocracy and caesaropapism, but also of their external signs, symbols, and sacraments— the politicoreligious ceremonies of consecration, the anointing of the king, the use of holy oils for nonsacramental purposes, stories of royal charisms, and so on—all of which clearly contradict the spirit of the Gospel.

For and Against Democracy

Does this mean, inversely, that a republican or democratic system of government is exempt from all antievangelical ambiguity? Of course, always in the perspective of analogical transposition, we should point out correspondences: we may immediately remind ourselves, although it is not directly the issue here, of the separation of powers, the appearance of "laicity," which as doctrine, if not as antireligious manifestation, is completely in the evangelical spirit. Besides, we could also refer to the change from relationships of authoritarian dependence to those based on liberty, equality, fraternity, a greater sense of responsibility and work in common, and the free delegation of democratic power,[2] all of which substantively follow the direction of the evangelical revelation. In sum, the positive and the negative aspects of each of these opposed political systems are exactly contrary and in opposition.

But inversely, is not a republican form of government filled with dangers from the point of view of the Gospel? This hardly seems debatable. Among the principal points to be made in this context, we can hardly leave out the reflex of irreligion that almost automatically follows the breakup of a centuries-old clerical stranglehold on power; what is most serious is that it is perhaps not simply a de facto reaction that could be explained as due to historical reasons; there is a kind of frenzy of secular humanism that, in a confused but strict logic, is improperly transposed from the level of political systems to that of faith. The climax of this process is reached in a certain divinization of the State (as a moral person, a vicar, or a substitute of the physical person of the kings), a "hypostasis" that blends in with the apostasy of the masses that often accompanies it.

Active Indifferentism in the Direction of History

The first conclusion is obvious: the necessity for Christians to return to the indifferentism of the Gospel in regard

[2] In reality it would be necessary to distinguish between democracy and the republic; a monarchy can be democratic, as in England, where the king reigns without governing. In this case there remain simply those criticisms attached to the danger of the magical confusionism implicit in the monarchical principle. Inversely, Greek and Roman antiquity were familiar with undemocratic republics. Are they conceivable today? This is not the place to open a discussion on this point, which is nevertheless extremely important not only for the sociologist but also for the ordinary citizen.

to the forms of government, not allowing themselves to be confined within their supposed internal logic, is confirmed. Each of these systems presents difficulties in relation to the evangelical ideal, even when analogically transposed to the temporal order, but we also recognize valuable preparatory groundwork being laid of a complementary character, useful for the gradual construction of an earthly city that would so much more closely approximate the heavenly city —that is, the Kingdom—that after the Parousia the two would ultimately coincide. The Christian is therefore not entitled to oppose any of these forms of government as such.

Nevertheless, a corrective that is almost equally obvious immediately asserts itself: can we not make out an evolutionary line of development in the relationships that exist in regimes based on a descending and imposed authority and those in which authority comes from below and is accepted in liberty, equality, and fraternity? From Aristotle to Rousseau and all their descendants, philosophers and jurists have always had the habit of discoursing rationally in absolute terms on the relative value of different political systems, as if they were on the same level; and one could discuss their rational (or presumably rational) content in itself, without including a genetic factor. Nevertheless, the latter would seem difficult to ignore. It is hardly arguable that the two poles of monarchical and democratic power constitute—through centuries of opposition and misfortune, revivals and repetitions—the two limits of the political evolution of humanity. Everything seems to indicate this: not only the fact that the powers in which authority comes from above may be counted in decreasing numbers from the beginning of civilization to our time, but also the contemporaneity and connaturality of the magic mentality that was widespread in earlier ages, along with the monarchical political structure. Inversely, we see the growth of the positive mentality and of democratic structures.

On this foundation we might superimpose a particularly interesting consideration from our point of view: the parallel evolution of Revelation which, expressing itself first in the Old Testament in terms of a hierarchy of descent and authority, has passed through a radical mutation with the Gospel of the Lord; we have become adoptive sons, brothers, citizens of a world in process, children of God, "sharers in His nature." His people have become free. The trajectory of these convergent evolutions, which possess at least some presumptive value, would seem to make it almost impious for the Christian who wishes to live the Gospel to take up a position fundamentally opposed to modern political structures.

However this may be—and the essential is still the fundamental attitude of evangelical indifferentism—it is important to include an additional element that would make it active or positive. In fact, because the ultimate purpose in any case is the progress of humanity toward the final establishment of the Kingdom, the evidence has become apparent that there is a necessity for the evangelical Christian to work *within* the temporal regime in which he find himself in such a way that the difficulties and inherent dangers of the specific system are reduced or eliminated and the evangelical potentialities linked with it are brought to fruition. The particular emphasis of his effort, therefore, will vary, depending on the regime in which he finds himself; in one, both by his example and by more explicit witness, he ought to draw attention to the protection of various liberties (including those of the Church), of human dignity, justice and its rights, and the transcendence of the sacred; in the other, the emphasis will be more on the permanence and primacy of the demands of faith, the dangers in the magical worlds of substitution (cult of personality and of "stars") and of materialistic intoxication. And it will doubtless be more difficult for him, in spite of the fact that the terrain has theoretically been better prepared, to bring to this democratic world, more easily self-contained and satisfied with itself, the spiritual addition it needs (without being aware of this) if it is not to forget the essential.

In both cases, the Christian of the Gospel will find himself directly involved in the struggle over what is best in a particular system and in opposition to its limitations. Because these limitations are always registered in the direction of the least effort and the greatest number, the Christian will in any eventuality be a sign open to contradiction, just as it was announced and ordained by the Lord. In both cases, too, his role will ultimately be to see to it that the substance of real politics is transmitted by means of whatever formal political structures are in existence.

12

POLITICAL SYSTEMS AND ECONOMIC STRUCTURES

Right and Left

The consideration of formal political regimes has led us back to the genuine essence of politics. But we have seen that, in one sense and up to a certain point, analysis based on the Gospel is in agreement with the Marxist analysis on the radical and supreme importance of the real content of social relations, whether or not they are called economic. We must now proceed a little further. A terminology of relatively limited usage in space and time serves as a hinge between formal politics and genuine politics; despite its limitations, it is convenient and suggestive to speak about "right" and "left." It is indispensable to analyze this curiously corporeal and topological language within an evangelical framework before going further.

Although people are often ironical about the simplistic physical and topographical representation of "right" and "left," these terms constitute at present the only two points of stable and consistent reference for political life in many countries; the truth is that their implications are particularly rich, subtle, and sometimes extremely tangled. Thus, depending on the situation, we would be able to say instead of "right": conservative, liberal, reactionary, counterrevolutionary; and instead of "left": progressive, laborite, advocate of planned economy, socialist, reformer, revolutionary. Pushing this analysis a little further, we would be able to maintain, provisionally and in terms of ordinary customs, that the left by and large represents the "people," the "mass," the more "politically conscious" workers, the "proletariat," the "victims" of major economic trends, the poor, the alienated, and their supporters. The right, accordingly, would represent the establishment, the rich and the powerful, the "capitalists," the "bourgeois," all good "right-thinking" property owners who respect "law and order." The right looks back and wants to stop the movement of history or even bring it back to earlier stages; the left looks to the future, wants a change, and insists that "things begin to move." The right defends the established order, whereas the left considers it unjust and looks to a future order. The key words for the right are: order, stability, free economy, patriotism, nation, defense of the individual, army, duty, work, business enterprise; those of the left are: freedom, progress, organization, state, internationalism, culture, recreation, civil rights, justice.

By now we should begin to see that there is less reason than one might have thought for ridiculing the symbolic naïveté of the terms "right" and "left"; in fact, it would be worth the time to probe systematically the "psychosociology" of humanity in order to discover their solid foundations. At least we can point out here that the right—for example, the right hand—is clearly held in high esteem and favored in the human subconscious. Psychologists, as well as left-handed people themselves, are well aware of it, and it is worth remembering that we reproach someone for being gauche. Professor P. M. Schuhl has written a very interesting essay on the preeminence of the right hand in the work of Plato; the Bible shows us the right hand of God as the symbol of power and honor; and at the Last Judgment the just will be invited to take their place at God's right hand, while those who are condemned, the "goats," will be on the left. (Baudelaire saw this as a normal indication of the split between the race of Abel and that of Cain.)

In brief, it appears natural, for whatever reason, conscious or unconscious, that the "right" has become the place for the "haves," for those with a good conscience and those who are respectable—in other words, the just, those who think themselves or wish themselves just, who believe the established order and system to be just (or wish to think so) because that system and order has worked out well for them (unless they recommend another system that would suit them even better); while those who are perpetually hungry, the "wretched of the earth," the "damned," [1] find themselves rejected on the left.

Of course, people can object that everything is a lot simpler than this, because the right is quite plainly that part of the assembly that sits at the right of the president, and so on. Yes, but apart from the fact that such a right is extremely relative, because it receives its name in relation to the president who faces the assembly, it could equally be called left in relation to the assembly that faces the president. Thus, as soon as one turns around, everything is changed. In addition (which is hardly an argument, but merely a retort), the real problem is to know for what deeper reasons (conscious or unconscious) conservatives happen to be seated on the right of the president, like the just sit at the right hand of the Father; this is why we made

---

[1] It should be stressed that this extensive use of a well-known affective terminology is deliberate, for the unconsciousness of peoples is very important and filled with meaning; not juridical but richly connotative language expresses this meaning.

our brief incursion into psychoanalysis, which would seem to indicate that the terminology is not so foolish or shallow that clever people, who enjoy poking fun at it, do not also want to talk about it.

It must immediately be pointed out that we have gone through an important transition in our discussion; after starting with a right and a left that were hypothetical and relative, we are now able to talk about an absolute Right and Left, perhaps not rationally established but possessing a physical and affective reality and finding a profound resonance in the Gospel. If, in fact, it is true that there always have been and always will be poor people among us, for someone to be part of the left, in terms of absolute value, would be to make himself truly poor with those who are, regardless of what political system they are living under, the real poor, the victims, the damned. This would mean wishing their "salvation" and contributing to it; it would mean being hungry and thirsty for truth and justice, and for a kingdom that, according to Christians, is that of God and is to come "on earth as it is in Heaven." To be part of the right, on the contrary, is to regard oneself and the existing "order" as just, or sufficiently just; this would mean, finally, to justify oneself and not to recognize one's sin. In practice, we can recognize this attitude in the man who, with or without easy protestations of service and respect for the unfortunate, inevitably defends his own good and the acquisitions of all the satisfied and the well-fed. He eats his share of cake while finding it right that others have their dry bread or no bread at all; it is all justified by deciding that he is one of the good people, the chosen, and that the others are rabble. In sum, what we are dealing with is a subtle sublimation of the old theocratic error that suppressed the perspective of the Kingdom that is to come in favor of the Kingdom that has already been achieved. Christ does indeed place the good on the right and the wicked on the left "as the shepherd separates sheep from goats" (Mt 25:32). But the text that we are dealing with there has to do with judgment *after* the Parousia. Until then, no one is able to consider himself as good, as one of the sheep, firmly situated at God's right hand.

If we have really understood what is to be understood as the absolutes of Right and Left, it appears quite clear that they are not linked with any party or form of government, for they are to be found at a very profound level, both physical and affective, which cannot be expressed in juridical terms. There can, for example be a monarchist right or an oligarchical, democratic, republican, or even "revolutionary" right; it hardly matters—it is not the same policy (and the same holds true for the left). We can talk about a mentality of the right as soon as there is an open or even unavowed defense of the propertied classes (with the result that there can and does in fact exist a real right of what is nominally the left, and vice versa). But it is precisely in regard to this that there is terrible confusion in the modern mind, a confusion that is carefully maintained. In fact, by switching from the physical to the juridical, by drawing attention primarily to differences between juridical entities (systems of government) and then political parties, the essential opposition between the haves and the have-nots is avoided. In this way we can proceed smoothly from the monarchy to the empire, then to the republic, with revolutionary interludes, because what does it matter if money and power are discovered in the same hands at each stage? Rich and poor, representatives of the "established disorder" and those without power, through all these changes remain virtually the same. In each new situation, a handful of wretched men filled with goodness and human naïveté hope for a profound change, while the fortunate ones who benefit from the system simply change their clothes, their banners, and eventually the political system. It is hard to understand by what aberration, as a result of what intellectual confusion, so-called leftists continually assume that the republic or "democracy" or the "revolution" are, by virtue of their very name, necessarily of the "left" or more "leftist," in absolute terms, than any other system. The humble race of the poor, those who own little or nothing, know every well, with the wisdom of the common people, that all these great words are over their heads and that this kind of talk does not do anything to change their condition as victims. They know that the powerful will throw them a bone when their growls get too loud, but they have little respect for the fancy wrapping and the fine words.

The ancients—for example, the Romans—were a little more frank and revealed their positions quite plainly: on one side was the party of order, the good people, who were also people of property (*boni, optimates*), which today we would call the right, the liberal conservatives, whose great Roman leader in the republican era was Cicero (and there had also been Pompey in his first stage, Milo, and Octavius). On the other hand, there was the party of the people (the "populace"), the troublemakers, revolutionaries, roughnecks, the "filth of Rome" whose more or less avowed and more or less sincere leaders were, during the same republican period, a Caesar, a Clodius, an Antony—the left.

No one claims that the leaders of that party were usually sincere and loyal advocates of the disinherited, but at least the situation was made clearer and more closely approximated the impulses of the collective unconscious of which we have spoken because of this separation between these two very simple parties (a situation resembling that among the modern English who have remained worn down and little given to argument) and especially, we repeat, because of the extreme and cynical frankness of the "rightists," who exclaimed aloud to their fellows, in extremely serious

circumstances and in front of everyone, that the salvation
of the country depended on them, the good people, *boni*,
and on the protection of their property (*bona*). The Latin
terms are symptomatic of a certain basic mentality; today
no one would any longer, even in pragmatic England, dare
to express himself so crudely, whereas Cicero and his followers never tried to disguise their general orientation. The
Romans could be adequately and naturally divided into
two species (those who are well off, the rich, and those
who have nothing, the plebs, the poor, the common herd,
homines perditissimi); what was important was defending
the former against the latter: this is what was meant by defending the *republica*. If there is any question about this,
just re-read the orations against Catiline or the *pro Milone*;
that is what is called speaking frankly.

And what has happened since then? Is it true, as the
Marxist would argue, that the Christian revolution and
those who have followed it, who have brought to *all* men
the news of what should truly be called, despite all abuses,
a liberty, equality, and fraternity that would be radical and
absolute, have also served to blunt the power of the poor to
revolt? It does not seem that things are quite that simple.
For example, if we take the case of the Gospel, it is quite
obvious that this attempt to perfect the structures of the
thought and action of humanity did not immediately suppress the radical egoism of nature that has discovered the
clever resources of argumentative reason in order to be able
to remain satisfied under the cover of this very search for
perfection. (That is why Christians persist in saying that
no revolution will be truly effective if it is not also a revolution of the heart.) When a bacterium or some foreign
body penetrates an organism, the biologists tell us, the latter carries out a partial or general mobilization of its forces,
which will tend to the elimination, draining off, or even
assimilation of the foreign body; this is also what has taken

place in regard to, or rather against, the Christian virus. The elimination of the cross, of which Saint Paul spoke, has always been a terrible danger for the Church; and in the case in hand, for the rich and those who held to a comfortable paganism, it was an extremely advantageous undertaking to bring about a compromise between the new doctrines and age-old egoism, while transposing and subliminating genuine differences to the evanescent level of juridical ideas about political systems and parties. It is in this way, for example, that they have recently tended to believe and led others to believe that the "republic" and "democracy" defended the people (what would Cicero, that good republican, have thought about that?), while dictatorial and fascist regimes were necessarily conservative or part of the extreme right wing. Do we still need to be reminded that the Marxist revolution, which in its origins was a people's movement, has a dictatorial tendency and that fascist dictatorships (Mussolini, Hitler, Perón) have included a certain socialist and "populist" aspect that was not simply an illusion?

But we must go even further. In considering the lessons of the past, as well as certain characteristics drawn from psychological analysis, we are forced to recognize that if conservatives easily accommodate themselves with any type of government (from right-wing dictatorship to democratic republic), leftists seem to tend, almost inevitably, to "tyranny" in the Greek sense of the word—that is, in more modern terms, to the dictatorship of the proletariat— although today, embarrassed by the subtleties of language, they are or should be ashamed of this.

On this point, too, Greek and Roman antiquity furnishes us with valuable data. Obviously, one frequently encountered rightist dictatorships in those centuries when circumstances were favorable, but it seems that most of the time conservatives proved themselves partisans of the republic, with its system of representation tailored to their measurements, while "the people who had nothing" placed their confidence in the hands of a "tyrant."

We are not saying that "tyranny" is essentially part of the absolute left but only that in fact it was generally an instrument employed in efforts at practical realization of policies closely identified with the left (which does not mean that it was not often if not always utilized by cynical men hungry for personal power). Unfortunately, this tendency of the leftist movement is easily enough explained at the level of the collective unconscious: in fact, because the masses of the people have always been more or less sacrificed no matter what government was in existence (bourgeois or rightist dictatorship, classical monarchy or republic), the existing government is always "the established order" that has again become unjust. In consequence, every strong man who rose up against this order, whether or not he was sincere, if he knew how to show the poor their own wretchedness and how to give expression to their demands, has inevitably awakened a considerable echo among the people. Note well that we say: every strong *man;* the same is not true of a system of government or some political-legal entity, for the poor have special need of a Messiah, a Defender, an Incarnation, a Redeemer, a promise of salvation incarnate. Moreover, this situation is quite logical, because ultimately the extraordinary individual who becomes hardened least quickly is also one who will least quickly create a new established order that is again unjust. But it always seems to happen in the end: an administration, a whole system, come together around the man, and we fall again into a regime or a substitute for it; we get far away from concrete reality and forget the concrete aspirations of the disinherited. Instead, we construct beautiful principles and make complicated laws; or again, the tyrant himself grows defensive, comes to lean more and more on the right, and either turns into a bourgeois dictator [2] or founds a dynasty.

In sum, the people are always ultimately deceived and disappointed; the tyrant who represented the aspirations of the poor, who promised the full-scale shake-up, the suppression of the established order, himself becomes an established order. The result is that the left—which, in order to be truly left and truly of the people, finds itself most of the time almost inevitably led to tyranny—falls back again inevitably into a bourgeois dictatorship, or a monarchy, or a democratic republic, into the administration of outmoded structures. (It is the grandeur of anarchist thought to have perceived this and tried to avoid it.)

Thus, it is not enough to speak of evolution or of revolution in order to be "popular"—that is, to be truly of the left; revolution can become bourgeois in the proper sense of the word, just like dictatorship. Indeed, such a development at first seems inevitable when we take into consideration that the law of least effort is universal and that the law of the destruction of energy is not valid only for the physical sciences.

If the left wishes to be faithful to the people and to the poor, it must constantly guard against becoming established and simply protecting its own "order." "Revolution" is a word; to be truly and constantly revolutionary, revolution ought to be permanent, continually in motion. Therefore it seriously needs a principle that is absolutely superior to man; for man naturally, because of his nature, grows tired, becomes bored, turns middle class, begins to feel righteous, and decides that everything is all right as long as he is doing all right. Would this higher principle, at once transcendent and immanent, be history on the march, as many men to-

---

[2] This is indeed the case, it would seem, of Marxism-Leninism-Stalinism. See the fine study of H. Chambre, *Le Marxisme en U.R.S.S.*

day think and hope? We do not believe so, because history
is not the principle but only the expression, the outer film
of this constant surge of activity that is revolution.

What is this principle that is superior to man? "Man infinitely surpasses man," Pascal wrote on a scrap of paper.
Yes, through the Son of Man, who has come to save and
redeem not the just and the respectable but those who were
lost—the poor and the sinners.

Several conclusions seem called for after this hasty
sketch of the effective and popular representations of right
and left. First of all, we see that in spite of their primitive
aspect, if we give them their full meaning (which we have
called absolute), they can help us penetrate into political
realities that are more concrete, more real—and consequently, more evangelical—than the terminology used to
describe various systems of government. Here it is no
longer a matter of formal politics, so it is quite natural that
the Gospel judges things differently; the evangelical spirit
cannot be harmonized with a right-wing mentality,
whether it be cynical (as with Cicero) or hypocritical (like
our own), because it cannot defend money and property
or "good people" or the ideal of comfort that ignores—in
reality if not in word—those who live in discomfort. Is this
to say that the Gospel canonizes the left? Hardly, for it
will constantly upbraid the left, both for its own hypocrisy
when it pretends to have accomplished what it has not and
for its constant tendency to permanently install itself in
power and its very human temptation to violence (tyranny, dictatorship) in order to accomplish its purposes.
The Gospel asks us to be unconditionally and absolutely on
the side of the poorest of men, those who are most unfortunate, the most disinherited; [3] if this means to be part of

_____

[3] Obviously this does not mean that we should unconditionally
approve those who intoxicate the poor with a false ideology, even
if the poor follow them.

the left, as it seems, then the Gospel is leftist—not abstractly, but in terms of concrete reality, everyday caring for people. The Gospel tells us that only our interior transformation (according to the law "Seek first the Kingdom"), only our life by, with, and in Christ can produce these fruits *ad extra*, and the communist experience tragically and unconsciously proves it right. "The poor you will have always with you" is not a phrase that implies any kind of hypocritical resignation, but the rejection of self-satisfaction and any kinds of establishment. Only the Gospel of the Lord is truly of the left; to our unhappiness and our shame, we Christians have left it truly alone.

13

CAPITALISM AND SOCIALISM

By penetrating, if not more profoundly at least more rationally, the real structures of politics, we find the modern expression of its economic level in terms of capitalism and socialism as a specific form of the opposition between right and left.

It is expedient, when we speak of capitalism, to be reminded that it is also called economic liberalism, doubtless for the reason that this makes for an orderly symmetry in contrast to the planned economy of the socialist or socializing state, but the whole problem is still to know what is free in this free economy—is it man, or is it money? Because capitalism is not a religion or a philosophical doctrine, the answer is obvious: through free enterprise, free property, free exchange, what is free is money. It is true that, rationalizing because of a more or less conscious shame, the defenders of the system insist that this freedom of money involves the freedom of man, who because of it can, without constraint, use his gifts and possessions for his material and spiritual well-being, develop himself on every level, and gain the position to which his abilities allow him to aspire.

In fact, however, it is not necessary to insist a great deal before we remember that the freedom of money influences both men who are owners and men who labor (with no necessity that they be the same) and that it results in a new and polymorphic form of slavery, with the latter chained to their job and the former delivered over to their money. The supposed human liberty that capitalism celebrates, therefore, is most often illusory, tending more to what philosophers called the freedom of indifference than to the freedom of determination. Both those alienated by money and those alienated by work are in fact dragged into a vicious deterministic cycle, from which they are unable to emerge Christianly except by great effort—for the owners, by rejecting the system, and for someone who is a worker, by spiritually eliminating it.

On this whole subject, in contrast to the cases of those governments that depend on power, the Gospel cannot and does not remain indifferent. This kingdom of money and this degrading freedom, both in its hypocrisy and in its fruits, are eminently antievangelic; a strange darkening of the Christian conscience was required for people to be able to think that this choice of a system of economic organization was free, even if one of the alternatives depended on the enemy of the Kingdom, Mammon.

Obviously this does not mean that the Gospel is necessarily socialist, if only by virtue of the logical rule in regard to the relationship of contrary terms, which, unlike contradictories, can both one and the other be false. It is necessary, therefore, to look at things a little closer. Socialism can be essentially characterized by economic organization and planning, the common ownership of the means of production, an active will to give each man an equal opportunity and to constantly improve the material condition of human communities.

We may conclude from this that socialism thus manifests a certain harmony with the Gospel, notably in its suspicion of money values, its communitarian spirit extending to all humanity, and its concern for justice.[1] Would the Church then be falling into sin once again by antievangelism because it perseveres in pointing out its differences with so-

[1] It is often by comparison with a particularly orthodox form of capitalism that socialist economics displays its relatively more Christian values. For example, a practicing Christian whose sincerity is unquestioned wrote a book that discusses the history and economics of coffee, constantly pointing out that social progress and a greater concern for man, for the poor, and for justice contradict the economic prosperity of the country. All the horrors of the nineteenth century are apparently forgotten: the subjection of a part of humanity—men, women, and children—to the profit of the owners, twelve- and even eighteen-hour working days, child labor, and so on; all this is forgotten in a lyrical celebration of a stable currency and an active market. All this is presented tranquilly, calmly, without the least suggestion of bad conscience, without the smallest footnote to show that the author was aware that this one-way "prosperity" was achieved at the price of blood, the blood of the poor.

This is a special case of conservative mythology regarding "order." Everything should be in order: the street, the country, the currency, the budget—but what kind of order? Those who speak this kind of language and claim to be Christians should be asked directly: have you reflected on the fact that as a consequence of being Christian you ought to follow the precepts of the Gospel regarding the poor, justice, and the Kingdom of God? Must you not choose between God and Mammon, and have you not already chosen Mammon, prosperity, and its order? Do you not realize that everything must be subordinated to what is essential—the Kingdom of God and His justice; anything else is secondary— human success, equilibrium, harmony, the beauty (!) of order and money? Consequently, it should be of no importance to Christians that money is less stable if there is also less poverty. Which do you consider closer to the Gospel: the man who claims that order, stability, and economic prosperity have first priority even if that means that a certain percentage of the population will be unemployed or live in destitution, or the man who believes that it is possible to work for the satisfaction of human services and the aspirations of all in a renewed economic order?

cialism and the reserve it feels for various socialist regimes? We believe that if there has been a failure of evangelical spirit in the Church, it is perhaps in not sufficiently conceding—indeed, it would often seem, not conceding at all—the profoundly Christian dimension of socialism, rather than in criticizing what can rightly be criticized: its positivistic, atheistic, and materialistic aspects; its concern with only the social organization of humanity; and its destruction of man's freedom. In my opinion, these objections have a foundation in fact. If its atheistic positivism is partially explained historically in terms of the origins of socialism, the fact remains that precisely because of its great accomplishments socialism is more inclined than any other system that has ever existed to the temptation of a pagan and materialistic atheism; and this has resulted, among other things, in its tendency to standardization, proselytization, and devaluation of the individual.

But all this is profoundly against the spirit of the Gospels: for Christ, each man has his own unique and extraordinary destiny. The Gospel, profoundly communitarian, has discovered the equilibrium of man in society by means of its theory of the Kingdom in the process of being built. Here we come back to the famous sentence "Seek ye first the Kingdom of God, and all these things will be added unto you." Turning that proposition on its head and seeking first "what will be added," socialism finds itself driven, from a number of different directions, into various impasses.

In fact, we would readily extend, in the name of the Gospel, the criticism of socialism much further than the Church does officially (which, perhaps, in this case does not go far enough in its concern for evangelism). Man's freedom is not the only area in which the bankruptcy of socialism is manifest, for socialism remains quite timid concerning money, which the Gospel scorns, downgrades, and

prefers to know nothing about.[2] The inadequacy of socialism is equally evident in regard to equality; no socialist
country or party has decided to reward men simply according to their needs and the relative quality of their work instead of in terms of their functions.[3] Nevertheless, as soon

[2] Let us not be too quick to denounce this as utopian or sentimental daydreaming and naïve primitivism. At the present time
there are a few extremely reputable economists (socialist in tendency) who seriously propose (moreover, for technical reasons,
not in the name of the Gospel) to do away with computing national and international wealth in terms of money (whether gold
reserves or bank notes) and replace it with an estimate of a country's capacity for the production of consumer goods. Such a system of measurement, among other advantages, would offer fewer
impediments for those nations in the process of economic and in-
dustrial development.

In the time of slaves, the abolition of slavery was considered
a sentimental daydream by all those men who considered themselves serious and practical; the struggle for equality was looked
at in the same way.

[3] The social problem presented by the organization of indus-
trial work, to which both neocapitalism and socialism—each in its
own way—try to offer an answer, is not simply a matter of the
better distribution of wealth. It is also a question of assigning responsibility, on every level.

A typical management attitude is expressed in the statement
of French owners (*Centre national du patronat français*, February
1965) that "authority cannot be shared." This is in strict contradiction with recent encyclicals that have insisted that workers no
longer be treated "as passive and silent performers" but that they
be called upon to participate not only in the fruits of the enterprise
(especially in auto-financing) but even in its ownership and management.

"The workers and those who represent their rights, their demands, their aspirations, ought to be present not only in the interior of each productive organism but in the public authorities and
regional, national, and world institutions in which the decisions
are made that affect economic and social life," wrote John XXIII
in *Mater et magistra*. He did not hesitate to continue: "Advancing
in the footsteps of our predecessors, We consider as legitimate the
aspiration of workers to take an active part in the life of those
enterprises in which they are engaged and perform their work."
It would not be difficult to discover an evangelical foundation

as primary emphasis is given to human fraternity and the profound equality of men beyond any question of individual gifts, opportunities, and education, it can seem *unjust* to favor the man who has conceived a plan more than the one who executes it. The laborer who works hard, doing all that he can do, is not merely the equal and the brother of the engineer who has also drawn on his own gifts as completely as possible: he has done as much as his brother.

In short, we always arrive at the same conclusion: socialism (like the left, like democracy) will be evangelical or will not come into being; its difficulties find their explanation and their solution in the Gospel.

Indeed, it would be advisable to explain more nuances of meaning and to be more prudent; but we cannot, in any strict sense, speak of evangelical socialism except to the degree that it prepares the road to something else. In the same way that socialism has marked a step forward in the political development of men, so tomorrow our children will know an economic structure even nearer to the Gospel, more just, more free, more truly fraternal, one that will

for this requirement; the Incarnation of the Son of God and the deification of men that it implies in terms of the universal "recapitulation" of all things in Christ demand that we strive to promote at once the dignity of persons, their moral elevation, and their reconciliation without the suffocation of mob rule. "It is necessary to work so that the enterprise becomes a community of persons in the relationships, the functions, and the situations of its entire personnel."

Here we have a touchstone that allows us to judge the whole system, whether neocapitalist or socialist, with another criterion than that of the distribution of consumer goods.

"If the structures, the everyday functioning, and the overall atmosphere of an economic system tend to compromise the human dignity of those who are involved in it and to systematically weaken their sense of responsibility and present an obstacle to their personal dignity, such an economic system is unjust, even if, by hypothesis, the wealth that it produces reaches a high level and is distributed according to the rules of justice and equity" (*Mater et magistra*).

nevertheless take more and more into consideration, within the continued autonomy of its temporal organization, the primacy of the quest for the Kingdom of God. This will be a new stage on the way to the Parousia; whatever its name is, Christians ought to be the first to get there. Will they?

14

CONCLUSION:
Propositions for Action

The ancients were wrong to link the Word of God in its political realization to a particular form of society. Nevertheless, they possessed, better than we do, the sense of the absolute nature of God and his Word. A politics drawn from Holy Scripture was natural for them, whereas today the very idea has become scandalous and unintelligible.

We have practiced an unfortunate split between our religious life and our political life, between the Church and the everyday world, between the active Christian spirit and sacramental practice.

With fingers burned by the pretensions of theocracy, on guard against the confusion that still exists in that area, fearful of being called clericalists or being accused of obscurantism, and not wanting to seem hypocritical in their own eyes, the majority of Christians today seem perfectly willing to accept the formula that they can be "good Christians in regard to their personal and interior life but completely free and independent as regards their choices in the secular city."

In their distrust, which has been of long standing, of

anything that might resemble a Christian politics (both the word and the thing), they have come to confuse, as Joseph Folliet has said, "the social thought of the Church with a purely natural morality and natural law. In other terms, do they not reduce the social thought of the Church to natural morality?" Folliet added, "The social thought of the Church integrates natural morality and natural law, but adds to it the evangelical revelation with all its terrible demands. We must not forget it." [1]

Who then is right, the ancients or the moderns? It would be better to say that both have useful reminders for our present purpose: the former because of their desire not to abdicate the duties of Christians, the latter in their insistence that we not take the name of God in vain. These two contradictory intentions have their weakness and their grandeur. The weakness of the ancients was that they did not see that they were making God blaspheme, making him lie, attributing intentions to him that he could not have. The weakness of the moderns was to reserve the area of politics to man alone and, through a kind of austere sense of modesty, keep God away from it.

The evangelical synthesis of this kind of Hegelian dialectic was nevertheless quite simple at its origin, and the first Christians sensed it very well: for Christians, nothing happens without God, and nothing can escape his evangelical word; but the point of insertion of this word into politics is

---

[1] One could object that John XXIII in *Mater et magistra,* and even more in *Pacem in terris,* voluntarily placed his argument on the level of natural law and natural morality and that this is surely one of the reasons for the extraordinary welcome given to these encyclicals by "men of good will," both believers and unbelievers, to whom they were addressed. Nevertheless, the evangelical substratum of these documents emerges, sometimes even quite openly, in these central statements of a pope who appeared to everyone as haloed with an evangelical "aura."

still required, and this does not mean its external form but its political reality.

What then ought we to do? What propositions for action seem called for?

Six Propositions

First proposition: Our first proposal for action has to do with religious knowledge. There is no paradox in this: action and effectiveness belong to those who have clear ideas. But it is striking to see to what extent, from the beginning, Christian political thought has lagged behind speculative thought and other areas of religious thinking, on the level of both the magisterium and the theologians. In fact if not in theory, Christian intellectuals, the fathers of the Church, and the theologians have allowed Christian thought to become disincarnate and have not seriously studied practical thought and politics. They have thus let it go astray when they have not themselves gone astray (we are thinking here of Vasquez and other Jesuit theologians of the Counter Reformation) in disastrous experiments at caesaropapism and theocracy. After all, action does not wait, and therefore the Church and its men of action—popes, bishops, and various leaders—were led to take up various positions. In general, then, we can say that there has been all too little study given to the meaning of a genuine political incarnation of the Gospel. The Fathers, bent on making the new faith be seen in a sympathetic light, at the risk of softening its sharp angles, proceeded to define the basis of faith; the theologians of the Middle Ages took up the relationship between faith and knowledge. Almost all the definitions of the magisterium deal with this area.

What is needed, therefore, is the undertaking and development of studies on scripture, the history of the Church, the fathers, the theologians, and the magisterium—from the political point of view, to see what can be extricated from them that is sure, probable, uncertain, or dubious. Nor can we forget to determine the doctrinal bearing of various papal and conciliar decisions (for example, what is the validity of the Syllabus of Errors?). It would be useful to have each of these, like each thesis, given a theological rating: a matter of faith (defined, revealed, implicit), close to faith, theologically certain, and so on. We cannot neglect anything that is capable of bringing light and certitude to action.

In the same spirit, and in parallel fashion, studies are needed of conflict between the imperatives of the politics of Christ and the data furnished by contemporary experience; for example, we still do not possess a solid comparative study of Christianity and socialism.

Second proposition: Let every Christian, and the Church itself, truly renounce in concrete terms every form of theocracy or hidden caesaropapism—that is to say, every transposition (whether on the political level, in the control of the labor movement, or whatever) of the dreams of the eagle with two heads, the two swords, the holy empire, into modern "Christian societies," more or less cleverly camouflaged, more or less unconscious.

To avoid even the appearances of collusion, we would wish Church authorities to keep a greater distance from civil authorities (although neither group can ignore the other), including public manifestations and liturgical acts ("official masses," and so on).

Third proposition (corollary): Instead, let every Christian and those Christians formed and brought up in the Church and in various ecclesiastical movements who have gathered together in churches offer their witness and become active wherever they are—as leaven in the dough, actively present everywhere—without reorganizing in their various milieus as confessional ingroups (political parties, unions, or movements that would be more or less officially or officiously Christian). Let us remind ourselves once more than neither Christ nor the earliest Christians set up political groups to act politically as Christians in the world; their political action in society was the *immediate* application, the efflorescence in action, of the demands of faith.[2]

Fourth proposition: Pastors think of informing themselves as to the principles of evangelical politics, and of preaching them, in churches and in various church-related movements, as well as bearing witness to them by their life.

Fifth proposition: As a consequence, let each Christian and all Christians nourished by the same bread and the same teaching bear the same judgments, take the same actions, in the same critical situations.

"Nourished by . . . the same teaching"—this means, in addition to our fourth proposition, that on major occasions pastors should not hesitate to remind the faithful very concretely, *ex cathedra,* with urgency and precision, in the face of immediate events and real problems, of the practical demands imposed as a direct and immediate consequence of evangelical imperatives.

Of course, this will be called neotheocracy; there is an instinctive fear of clericalism as soon as one refers to "instructions" on political matters given officially by the clergy. But such name-calling and suspicion is completely inappropriate in the present instance. Theocracy ties the spiritual to formal politics. But real politics has been di-

---

2 Are not Catholic action movements already tending in this direction by means of a policy of "regrouping," which allows members from various political and social backgrounds to rediscover themselves in the search for a renewed understanding of faith? Do they not understand the necessity—in order that something genuine take place—of being engaged in formal institutions that are inevitably imperfect, which the Christian should try to perfect from within?

rectly imposed by Christ. In the same way that a bishop or a parish priest might be led, for example, to recall *the* truth (there are not two of them) on the Incarnation or in regard to cosmic voyages and the plurality of worlds, similarly he ought to recall the basic data of evangelical politics on every important occurrence. A man cannot be a Christian, for example, and at the same time maintain that the peoples of the Third World can be left to death or servitude or that workers always have enough to live on, or that money has its own laws that must be followed. No ingenious distinctions between the speculative and the practical orders can have any real validity against such fundamental understanding of human priorities. Who can say how much harm has been caused by these distinctions and subdistinctions, as well as by the presumed political freedom of the Christian, which is completely illusory, having been surreptitiously transferred from the level of formal politics, where alone it should reign, to that of real politics.

In the latter domain, we would say that a political problem would have to be quite minor before the opinion of Christians can diverge. Even then, disagreements would be rather a matter of fact than of right and be seen as due to the difficulty of estimating in practice the hierarchy of values that, if they could be immediately recognized, would impose a choice.

But when it is a question of all the great problems—of being for or against a particular war or disarmament treaty or violent act; for or against such an effect of the reign of money or a particular stage of the union of men against the divisions of class, race, caste, and nation; for or against fraternity, liberty, equality, and so on whether one likes it or not—there is a Christian political orthodoxy, just as there is an orthodoxy on the Trinity and the Incarnation.

This does not mean that it is not important to recognize the complexity of political problems. We understand quite

well that the passage from evangelical inspiration to concrete applications does not often take place without hesita-
tions, obscurities, and often surprising detours. We are
justified in distinguishing four stages of this perpetual dialectic: first, there is evangelical inspiration, absolute in
character and penetrating everywhere; this inspiration is,
then, able to be expressed in principles that are also absolute
but are already abstract (for example, giving first place to
the poor or a distrust of money); these are the two stages
that we have tried to deal with in this brief inquiry. However, these principles that emanate from evangelical inspiration should inevitably be elaborated as a doctrine that, at
the same time that it tends to the absolute, will necessarily be
partial and relative to the degree that it represents the re-
fraction, in specific times and in concrete circumstances, of
the principles of the Gospel; this is exactly what the social
doctrine of the Church ought to be. Finally, this social doctrine results in concrete applications that are not always
necessarily coextensive and adequate to it.[3]

These distinctions, however valuable, far from reassuring
Christians ought to stir them to criticize more strictly—in a
sort of *praxis* of love—the adequacy of their political acts
as a response to the inspiration of the Gospel.

[3] The evangelical inspiration, both in its principles and in its
doctrine, does not prevent the man of action from analyzing concrete situations, their contexts and components, possibilities and
impossibilities, and from estimating the efficacy of the various ap-
proaches he may use and among which he may have to choose,
while running the danger of being wrong in good faith. It is with
a recognition of all this that he must work out a specific response
in each case.

Because the knowledge of these contingent elements, which
are so complex, is largely dependent on intellectual capacity, overall competence, and available information, it is not always morally
scandalous that Christians, all of whom desire to remain faithful
to the inspiration of the Gospel, have in practice responded in a
variety of ways that nevertheless are not objectively faithful to the
Gospel.

Sixth proposition: Let the bishops not condemn the position of those Christians who are called interiorly to take a precept of the Gospel literally and draw from it, as far as it concerns them, an exacting concrete application (which also represents a minority and revolutionary response), as in the case of absolute nonviolence, the refusal to bear arms; let Christians as a whole, instead of censuring their brothers or treating them as fanatics to be tolerated, look at them with respect and attention and say to themselves that this unusual conduct is perhaps the effect of a charisma through which we are all finally being challenged, in the depths of our conscience.

The Gospel of Christ, and not simply a reference to a purely humanitarian ideal, demands of us Christians a Christian action in the midst of the world, but without our getting together for that purpose in some confessional in-group. The extrication of Catholics from all clericalist, theocratic, and politico-confessional confusions calls for a commitment that is not optional, an involvement in all the great issues before which Christians cannot remain neutral: war, violence, social justice, housing, hunger, racism, child care, illiteracy, and so on.

The timidity of the Church in involving the faithful in political reality is disturbing to all men of good will. Moral rearmament, against which the hierarchy has rightly warned Catholics, has met with an acceptance precisely because of this failure. It is obvious that there was a great deal of naïveté involved in the continuing adventures of theocracy and caesaropapism in an improper linking of the spiritual and the temporal; nevertheless, even these historical errors manifest a recurrent need and a true intuition: there must be an outlet of faith in politics. We also rediscover this need, in even more frantic form, among the Jehovah's Witnesses, who frankly adopt the theocratic solution in the pure state and whose success among poor and simple people is well known.[4] Following their logic to the end, they do not shrink from adopting a fundamental position of conscientious objection to all war. Do we, who consider ourselves enlightened, have the same courage?

It is proper to correct any excessive sharpness that our remarks may contain with the application of an evangelical parable: "The Kingdom of God is like the father of a

---

[4] In a resolution taken up at their congress on August 1, 1958, the Jehovah's Witnesses declared "that the only stable government in the world is the Kingdom of God installed from this moment and placed in the hands of His anointed Son, Jesus; that no government of the Christian world has the support of God, since the Almighty sustains His own government, the Messianic kingdom, and the various Christian governments are destined to perish at His hands in the universal war of Armaggedon in which His reigning king will fight against them and against all the other parties of the Devil's organization, both human and spiritual. . . . That in its fear of atheistic communism and of another world war, the clergy has turned its back on Jesus Christ and given its support to political institutions destined to prolong this old world that is God's enemy, such as the League of Nations and the organization that has succeeded it, the United Nations; that the clergy has encouraged the people to make itself idols of these human substitutes for the Kingdom of God; that, through these projects inspired by the wisdom of this world and whose intent is to protect the people from a new and devastating world war by means of these powerless organizations, the clergy is not helping men to find a sure protection against an even more destructive war, 'the war of the great Day of the all-powerful God' (Apoc 16:14, 16); the result is that in times of international peace, the clergy exhorts the nations hypocritically not to make war, not to fight against men; but by giving support to human political projects, it encourages them to fight against God now and in the forthcoming war of Armaggedon. . . . That our earthly organization is theocratic, because it is ruled by the most high God, who is above us; that our chief, under the direction of God, is not a political dictator but our true shepherd, Jesus Christ; and that the Holy Scriptures are our manual of law, teaching, and higher education."

Obviously, it is much easier to smile at such a jumbled declaration, in which theocracy, and hence infidelity to the Gospel, sinks into the absurd, than to interrogate oneself about one's own responsibilities for such a state of confusion.

family who draws out of his treasure both new and old." The Gospel is a total treasure, given once and for all; but we shall never be able to complete the inventory of its gems. Some of them—for example, the transcendence of the real loyalty that one owes to one's country—can be expected to sparkle in all its brilliance only at the end of an evolution of the world's structures, an evolution in which, moreover, the Gospel has played its part. In addition, there are probably other gems that have not yet been uncovered.

In any case, it should by now be solidly established that Christians are consecrated, whether they like it or not, to the establishment in concrete terms of a universe of gentleness, freedom, and universal fraternity marked by the rejection of money and the love of the poor. In the same way that many priests are, quite properly, beginning to refuse the sacraments to those for whom they are only social rituals without any vital significance, it would not be wrong for those who, by action or omission, do not wish to incarnate the Gospel politically as it ought to be to come to the realization that they should exclude themselves. To be a leavening force in the world and make it rise, it is necessary not that Christians be numerous but that they be authentic.

Even if they were reduced to the point that they were again only a "small flock," Christians ought to believe in the strength that is in them while overcoming any temptation of aristocratic pride that would make them a sect. It must never be forgotten that God "wants everyone to be saved and reach full knowledge of the truth. For there is only one God, and there is only one mediator between God and mankind, himself a man, Christ Jesus, who sacrificed himself as a ransom for them all" (1 Tim 2:5–6).

EPILOGUE:
A Just Violence?

We need to return to an issue of burning actuality, one on which all of us who call for a deeper sense of political commitment need to reflect soberly and profoundly. A tragic question must be asked: is there a good as well as an evil violence? For myself, I believe the truth is indivisible: the assasinations of Gandhi, Martin Luther King, and the Kennedys; the wars in Vietnam and Algeria; and the H-bombs of America, France, and Russia do not exhaust the evil of violence. On the other hand, the guerillas in Latin America, the Chinese atomic potential, and violent student revolts in France and the United States are to be commended because they are revolutionary.

Today, however, we more and more frequently encounter the preaching of violence, not simply by racists and imperialists, but by those claiming to speak in the name of Christ's Gospel. Newspaper accounts refer to the case of an American Maryknoll priest who described the existing situation in Guatemala as such an obvious and prolonged tyranny that it justified tyrannicide and recourse to violent insurrection. A priest-professor at the Gregorian University of Rome, again with the situation in Latin America in mind, recently declared that when an illiterate population has not developed sufficient political maturity to bring about the existence of democratic institutions, there is only one way of changing the situation: "an unjust violence could not be thrown off except by a just violence." Theologians are increasingly being asked for a theology of just violence; perhaps the most widely known case is that of Camillo Torres, the priest-guerilla of Colombia, who is widely invoked as the first martyr of the Christian revolution in Latin America.

The deep generosity, the just aim—and unfortunately, the lamentable confusion—of this contemporary attitude is well expressed in a statement on Christianity and revolution signed by representatives of a number of well-known Catholic organizations:

The violence which reigns in our western world, the systematic exploitation of men and nations by the capitalist system under all its forms, and the impossibility of resolving the internal contradictions of this system by its own laws of evolution or by gradual reforms—these constitute objective conditions calling for revolution. But the subjective conditions for revolution depend on the will of men who collectively commit themselves to carry it out. Revolution appears to us as the only possible approach, and implies a radical change of economic and political structures, but there will be no structural revolution without cultural revolution.

We are quite aware that this revolution calls Christianity itself into question as regards its forms of thought, expression and action. But we are convinced that our commitment must be on behalf of oppressed classes and peoples working for their liberation in France and throughout the world.

The revolutionary struggle takes place in the perspective of the construction of the Kingdom of God without being identified with it.

As a community we express our support for those believers

who, because of their commitment, have been excluded from their local church and feel alone in their faith.[1]

Those who argue in this fashion seem to be totally unaware that they may be contributing—by word and action —to the growing contagion of violence. Curiously, many of them had long been fighting as I have—against the traditional theology of the just war. Now that the weight of opinion in the Church has shifted, as can be seen in the Second Vatican Council's declaration on modern war in the schema *On the Modern World* and in the increasing number of statements from influential bishops and theologians in many countries, they seem to have shifted ground and to adore the idol they helped to burn.

At least this is how I understand the position of Father Melville, the American Maryknoll missionary who champions the cause of violent revolution in Guatemala. Apparently he justifies his stand on the ground that the Church did not condemn the Crusades, or the two world wars, or the war in Vietnam. I would have thought this due to infidelity to the Church's evangelical mission. For him, it demonstrates that the Church accepts the idea of a just war and that the present situation in many areas of Latin America can be judged as one in which men may be right to take up arms to defend themselves. Indeed, we are beginning to find theologians proposing a theology of just violence; apparently the purpose aimed at can either sanctify or corrupt the violent action that is undertaken. This would imply that violence is good when it is employed to liberate oneself, and bad when it is simply a means of conquest. Un-

[1] *Le Monde*, March 3, 1968. This statement has been signed by the following groups: Témoignage chrétien, Christianisme social, Economie et Humanisme, la Lettre, Frères du Monde, Terre entière, Idoc, Commission des religions de la société africaine de culture.

fortunately, under the pressure of events, no one admits that he is waging a war of conquest, not even Hitler; it is always a war of liberation. If we are to be more than political partisans, we must face up to the possibility that the Lord's commandment is *absolute*.

If one considers subconscious motives, the advocates of just revolutionary violence can best be understood as driven by the need, probably unconscious, to feel morally comfortable. Their situation is not all that different from that of the Jesuit theologians in the Renaissance. After all, there is no reason to assume that those who developed the theory of the just war were simply stupid or hypocritical. On the contrary, it is because they were like ourselves, church-going Catholics with all the good will in the world, that they arrived at this aberration! Caught between the Christian imperative of love and the demand for justice (or what they conceived to be such) in regard to the defense and political organization of the new nations that were emerging, they believed that they had discovered a proper synthesis. Indeed, all betrayals of the Gospel by the Church are conceived on the same model.

Today, too, many of us find ourselves confronted by two evangelical absolutes, with justice or truth on one side, and love and non-violence on the other. I fully accept the leftist analysis of the destitution and injustice in Latin America, but as a declared partisan of revolution, I am convinced that this revolution should be a permanent one.

While recognizing the evangelical claims of desperate cases of injustice, I should also state that there comes a point at which many self-styled revolutionaries abandon the Gospel. They do not want to live with moral discomfort; confronted with the evangelical demands for justice *and* love, revolution *and* non-violence, they have neither the moral stamina nor the ascetic heroism to demand both and practice both, the former through the latter, and the latter through the former. They do not know how to achieve justice by non-violent means; they are not capable of saying, for example, that all Christians should go out to demonstrate in the street and that no one should move, but let themselves die there without a word, without a gesture, without protest, without drinking or eating, until major land reforms are instituted in Latin America, or until. . . . Apparently, at a given point, something in their unconscious decides that only one of the two imperatives needs to be heard in its full force, while the other—that of nonviolence—is subject to some kind of spiritual interpretation.

I cannot pretend to be basically different. I, too, have shown myself incapable of practicing both commandments. But I refuse to make myself comfortable and cover a basic contradiction, a permanent reason for an uneasy conscience. All of us must recognize ourselves as sinners before God every time we fail in this area and are unequal to the absolute claims of both justice and love.

This does not mean that we should ignore what a Camillo Torres has suffered—summoned by the old integralist cardinal of Bogotá, son of the dictator, driven to ask for a reduction to the lay state, massacred with his entire Christian maquis group almost without resistance in two weeks. I do not know exactly what I would have done if thrown into the situation of that amazing priest; I do know that, finding myself incapable of following the straight path of both resistance and non-violent revolution, if I had not followed him it would have been simply through cowardice. But I am also convinced that before the Lord I would have been wrong, that Torres was wrong and unfaithful to the Gospel. Only the non-violent are completely right.

But at least Torres lived his life, gave his personal witness as best he could, a just man and a sinner. That is quite different from righteously fabricating an up-to-date theology of just violence and remaining comfortably pious in the role of a suburban Che Guevara. We must insist on the right to do the wrong that one disapproves of and knows to be wrong, to suffer in the tension between two absolutes, and to try to come each day a little closer to the crucifying realization of these two commandments.

The defenders of violence, however, will use every sympathetic theme, every fashionable catch-word; they will even use the progress of theology as an argument for their position. In this perspective apparently the theologians of the just war were right in their time, and the spokesmen for peace were right a few years ago in Algeria; but the theologians of violent revolution are right today, at least in the case of the poor countries.

Nevertheless, this is to make a shambles of both politics and theology. If the theologian needs to elaborate his message *hic et nunc*, this does not neglect the absolute character of the Christian message which has been established in the Gospel and in the divine model should be imitated. There may not be many characteristics of this human absolute that can be enumerated, but the horizon to which it points surely includes absolute love and, therefore, absolute non-violence. If the theologian no longer affirms this horizon of total man, reconciled with God and in some way assimilated to him, he becomes the preacher of the rejection of God.

But the apologists for violence will not be easily convinced and are quick to suggest that non-violence may constitute the worst of violences since it is subtle and represents a hypocritical distortion of conscience. How can a man, they ask, tolerate a non-violent sacrifice even to the point of death, a fast maintained to the end, and the challenge that can be read in innocent eyes that glow with tenderness and resolution without fatally wounding his own soul?

Here we encounter in extreme form the old argument already familiar to the apologists of nationalist wars: after all, violence is simply part of life; the non-violent are fools and hypocrites. It will be necessary, therefore, for us to look at the idea of violence a little more closely.

It is certainly true that, speaking rather generally, violence is inseparable from life, but in a very ambiguous sense in which the idea of violence usurps the name and place of "reaction." In this sense, violence is the reaction—chemical, physiological, psychological, or social—to a stimulus; it is the reply to what the organism or the consciousness experiences as an aggression; in psychological terms, and on the level of the human being, it represents a certain type of reaction to a situation of frustration or stress.

It should immediately be recognized, however, that the higher one rises in the ladder of living beings or the more one advances on the temporal vector of evolution, the more this reaction is spiritualized. Purely chemical and physiological in the plant (which, for example, retracts or expands, depending on the sun), it becomes physiological or psychophysiological in lower and higher animals; flight or violent counter-aggression may indicate the defense reaction of the organism. In the case of superior vertebrates, more specifically primates, hominoides, and man, one observes that this defensive response, flight, or violent reaction (which constitutes one type of purely physical behavior, with bodily response, as indicated by some kind of gesture) has systematically been the lot of all the higher animals, probably up to and including the first specimens of homo sapiens: you hit me; I hit you, or run away.

A decisive step was made in the purging of violence when violent psychic behavior—whether verbal, mental, or

political (employing insult, resentment, or a constitutional
defense system)—succeeded violent physical behavior. Finally there appeared, first in exceptional persons or in
religious revelation, the non-violent psychical reaction that
rejected any feeling of hatred and excluded every response,
whether in speech or action, except that of love.

It is obvious that this succession is relative, that the brute
beast continues to exist to react as such, and that many men
persist in responding to aggression by blows, war, or flight;
the diffused "violence" of words, feelings, or institutions
remains the common lot of men, including myself. Nevertheless, a line of evolution has been sketched out through
the appearance of more spiritual reactions in the great
phylum of life.

To take an obvious example, if I step on a dog's tail, he
will howl, run away, or bite; I would expect similar and
more dangerous reactions from a chimpanzee. If I step on
the foot of one of my fellow-passengers in a rush-hour bus,
I may receive a punch, an insult, a groan, or, more rarely, a
smile of pardon. From the response of a blow to the firm
but open attitude of the non-violent man who will calmly
say, "You stepped on my foot on purpose. Why? I think
you must have something bothering you. Let's talk about
it," there is enormous progress. To simply insist that violence is inescapably intertwined with life and to fail to see
the difference between these various reactions is to deny
civilization and to abandon the pilgrimage of man to Christ,
who has established our true destination.

Indeed, to deny this progress is to deny Christianity.
And uniformly to designate as violence all possible
variations—war or physical violence, the insult or verbal
violence, unjust exploitation or political violence—is to
deny progress. Strictly speaking, we might reserve the term
violence for physical attacks and consider other forms as

violent only by analogy. They may well be hypocritical forms of violence, but hypocrisy, as we know, is the homage vice pays to virtue; hypocrisy may be the effect of civilization, but it is already a measure of progress when men are no longer able to act out their brutishness.

This is not to say that we can ignore or deny the appearance of surreptitious or analogous forms of violence. To take one particularly characteristic example, racism is one kind of almost reflex reaction, of verbal and mental violence, to aggression experienced as frustration.

If we return to my example of an incident on a bus in which someone's foot is stepped on, we notice in the defense reaction of the victim the perception of what in the aggressor appears most physically irreducible to his own nature. The next logical stage is the explanatory transferral of the aggression-frustration to this real or supposed peculiarity. In other words, if I am the victim, my "violent" unconscious tells me that this other could not be someone like myself, my brother, another myself; that would be too absurd and would be my destruction.

Hence, it is necessary that it be someone wholly other than myself, a non-brother, not a fellow creature, a non-man; although related to the naturalist class of men, he is rejected by me from the affective class of my fellows. If he speaks a foreign language and has olive skin, he is "a dirty half-breed"; if he has a German accent, he is "a dirty boche," if he talks through his nose, he is "a dirty Yankee." Tall or short, thin or fat, the same mechanism of verbal banishment comes into play. The feeling of racism consists in the defensive affirmation, mentally, verbally, or actively violent, of an "otherness."

The psychological root of racism is here; the illogical driver who transfers the cause of the accident to another car and places the blame on the fact that the other driver was a woman is being moved by the same psychic mechanism that drove Hitler to hold the Jews responsible for all the sins of the world.

The conclusion of all this is not that violence is inevitably part of life, but that man must sublimate the vital energy that exists in violence in a positive non-violence. Christians must realize that their role is not to teach the world violence, which it knows from birth, but to guide mankind toward its omega point, where there are neither tears, nor blood, nor war. Christ has revealed that man's true condition is peace. Unfortunately, most of us who call ourselves Christians prefer to accept the world's understanding of "realism," and although we may claim to admire the non-violent, we quickly add that their position is somewhat "escapist" and perhaps should be looked at as "merely prophetic." Such a tendency, which quickly opens the door to whatever savagery that wishes to claim the alibi of "legitimate defense," is well understood by Don Helder Camara, the noble archbishop of Recife: "Rather than go to the underdeveloped countries to bring them violence, stay in your own countries and convert men to justice and love. The Gospel is revolutionary in the sense that it demands our conversion to the love of God and the love of men. Be revolutionary like the Gospel, but without wounding love." [2]

We can only hope that those who wish to be Christian revolutionaries today will come to accept his counsel.

[2] A talk given in Paris, cited in *Le Figaro*, April 26, 1968.